ENDORSEMENT

We live in a post-Christian culture. Militant atheism is growing on the Internet. Immoral lifestyles are being normalized, and those who fail to conform are labeled as "judgmental," "intolerant," "unloving," and "(fill in the blank)ophobe." Some have even lost their jobs merely for expressing an opinion contrary to the new moral current. What is the proper response of the Christ-follower who desires to communicate the redemptive message of God's kingdom effectively yet without compromise? If you are looking for an answer to this question, you have picked up the right book. David Capes is respected all over the world for his fair and careful scholarship in the field of New Testament studies. But this volume is not an academic work. Capes leaves the classroom and invites you into his home where he shares wisdom gained from years of practical experience interacting collegially and on a regular basis with those of different faiths and world views. The pages of this book are filled with spiritual nuggets presented on a platter of winsomeness that readers will find both satisfying and effective. This book will guide you to become the effective witness for Christ you desire!

—Michael R. Licona, associate professor in theology,
 Houston Baptist University

Everyone wants to be popular, yet in the 21st century, popularity and church often can't fit in the same sentence. Why? David Capes roots out the problem and poses a wise solution. In *Slow to Judge*, Christians are challenged to be careful and thoughtful before taking positions and responding to the moral culture of the day. This lets the church respond firmly but in love and with compassion. It is the course the church should take, regardless of popularity. Yet if we do it right and well, we might just see popularity of the faith change in the eyes of the world.

—Mark Lanier, Lawyer, commentator, teacher, author of *Christianity on Trial: A Lawyer Examines the Christian Faith*

Working within his own deeply rooted Christian faith, Dr. Capes writes convincingly of how the wisdom of a "listening heart" can enable all human beings to meet each other with respect and love, while prizing their own and others' integrity, authenticity and difference.

—Muhammed Çetin, sociologist, congressman-Parliament of Turkey

How in the world, believing that Jesus of Nazareth is the full, perfect revelation of God, we Christians ever lapsed into judgmental, moralistic scolds, I'll never know. It's an offense against God, who meets us in Christ, for us to be known by many mainly for our judgmentalism. See? I'm already being judgmental against those who are judgmental! David Capes, in this lively, fresh, biblical, and insightful book helps us to take a good look at ourselves and to look at how we look at others, making us just a bit slower to judge and a great deal more eager to listen, to learn, and to welcome in the name of Christ.

—William H. Willimon, professor of the Practice of Christian Ministry at Duke University Divinity School, retired bishop of the North Alabama Conference of The United Methodist Church, and former dean of the Chapel at Duke University.

This book is needed. Winsome without being wimpy, Capes is a leader in interfaith dialog and a role model for me and for many others engaged in discussing our deeply held religious convictions. If Socrates were in Houston, I think he would be on Capes' radio program and enjoy this discussion.

—John Mark N. Reynolds PhD, provost of Houston Baptist University

Interfaith dialogue is usually no more than two monologues. David's very clear style, his stories and explanations, reminds me that true dialogue must begin with listening and understanding others through their own eyes, rather than through my own judgments. This is a great book that teaches and elevates the reader to a new understanding of what God expects of us!

—Stuart A. Federow, rabbi, Congregation Shaar Hashalom, Houston, TX and cohost of A Show Of Faith radio show

SLOW TO JUDGE

SLOW TO JUDGE

SOMETIMES IT'S OK TO LISTEN

BY DAVID B. CAPES

THOMAS NELSON
Since 1798

NASHVILLE   MEXICO CITY   RIO DE JANEIRO

Published in Nashville, Tennessee, by Thomas Nelson. Thomas Nelson is a registered trademark of HarperCollins Christian Publishing, Inc.

Page Design and layout: Crosslin Creative

Thomas Nelson, Inc., titles may be purchased in bulk for educational, business, fund-raising, or sales promotional use. For information, please e-mail SpecialMarkets@ThomasNelson.com.

Unless otherwise noted, Scripture quotations are taken from The Voice™ Translation. © 2012 Ecclesia Bible Society. Used by permission. All rights reserved.*

* Note: Italics in quotations from *The Voice* are used to "indicate words not directly tied to the dynamic translation of the original language" but that "bring out the nuance of the original, assist in completing ideas, and . . . provide readers with information that would have been obvious to the original audience" (The Voice, preface). Author emphasis in quotations from *The Voice* is indicated with the use of **boldface** type.

Scripture quotations marked NKJV are from THE NEW KING JAMES VERSION © 1982 by Thomas Nelson. Used by permission. All rights reserved.

Scripture quotations marked ESV are from the ENGLISH STANDARD VERSION. © 2001 by Crossway Bibles, a division of Good News Publishers.

Scripture quotations marked NRSV are from the NEW REVISED STANDARD VERSION of the Bible. © 1989 by the Division of Christian Education of the National Council of the Churches of Christ in the U.S.A. All rights reserved.

Scripture quotations marked NIV are from the HOLY BIBLE: NEW INTERNATIONAL VERSION®. © 1973, 1978, 1984, 2011 by Biblica, Inc.™ Used by permission of Zondervan. All rights reserved worldwide. The "NIV" and "New International Version" are trademarks registered in the United States Patent and Trademark Office by Biblica, Inc.™

Scripture quotations marked KJV are from the King James Version (public domain).

ISBN: 978-1-4016-8019-0

Library of Congress Cataloging-in-Publication Data
Capes, David B.
 Slow to judge: sometimes it's ok to listen / by David B. Capes.
   pages cm
 ISBN 978-1-4016-8019-0 (pbk.)—ISBN 1-4016-8019-4 (pbk.) 1. Listening—Religious aspects—Christianity. 2. Prejudices—Religious aspects—Christianity. 3. Religious tolerance. 4. Attitude (Psychology)—Religious aspects—Christianity. I. Title.
 BV4647.L56C37 2015
 241'.672—dc23

2015005083

Printed in the United States of America
15 16 17 18 19 20 [RRD] 6 5 4 3 2 1

For Rabbi Stuart Federow, Father Troy Gately,
Father Frank Rossi, Father Michael Barrett,
Bishop Oscar Cantu, Bishop Michael Olson,
Father Brendan Cahill, and Father Mario Arroyo.

Together you have taught me how to be
slow to judge and quick to listen.

TABLE OF CONTENTS

ACKNOWLEDGMENTS

In February 1991, I attended a Clergy Institute meeting at Congregation Beth Israel in Houston. I don't recall the topic of the day, but I do recall meeting a man who has become a dear friend. While standing in line with a colleague of mine, I struck up a conversation with Rabbi Stuart Federow. At the time, Federow was the Houston Hillel Director (Jewish student ministry coordinator at Rice University, University of Houston, and other Houston colleges). Since I was a new professor at Houston Baptist University, we had a good deal to talk about over lunch. The conversation continued after the Clergy Institute was over. On the way to my car, Rabbi Federow stopped me and asked a question: "David, would you like to be on a weekly radio talk show where a minister, priest, and rabbi compare religious perspectives on issues?" I thought the question was a little strange. It sounded like the beginning of a joke—a priest, a minister, and a rabbi walked into a radio station . . . . We had just met, but I said, "Sure, sounds like fun!"—expecting that nothing more would come of it.

Rabbi Federow had been bitten by the radio bug when he served as a congregational rabbi in Lancaster, California. In his spare time, he had been a frequent guest on a talk show called *Religion on the Line* hosted by Dennis Prager. It was essentially the same kind of show which Rabbi Federow described to me. Today, of course, Dennis Prager is a nationally syndicated talk show host and the author of several books, including *Why the Jews? The Reason for Anti-Semitism* and *The Nine Questions People Ask About Judaism*. In Prager, Rabbi Federow found a kindred spirit and hero, and he quickly became addicted to the talk radio format.

Over the next few years, the rabbi and I stayed in touch, having an occasional coffee or lunch together. But one day, the call did come. Stuart had been working behind the scenes with radio stations around Houston, advocating with several program directors for the kind of show Dennis Prager had hosted in California. In 1997, Roger Gray, who happened to be my favorite on-air personality in Houston, agreed to give us a try; so Stuart called me and said, "We've got a show!" After meeting with Roger and several test runs on other shows, *Faith Matters* aired its first show May 1997 on 97 Talk ("Houston's only FM talk station"). Now, seventeen years later, we've been on the air together for a total of twelve years.

Stuart and I wanted the show to have three co-hosts—a priest, a minister, and a rabbi—so we turned to the bishop of the Catholic Diocese of Galveston-Houston. Because Catholic priests are in short supply and very busy, Bishop Fiorenza decided to split the weekly duties among three priests who rotated throughout the month. Fathers Troy Gately, Frank Rossi, and Michael Barrett became our regular conversation partners during the early years of the show. From time to time, we'd invite representatives of other faiths— Hindu, Zoroastrian, Islam, Buddhism, Bahá'í, etc.—to be our fourth chair. But the regulars were the priest, the minister, and the rabbi. Given the nature of radio, we've had different names for the show and have been on different stations over the last seventeen years. The current version *A Show of Faith* airs weekly on 1070 AM KNTH The Answer. Our show is streamed live over the Internet, so we have listeners and callers from all over the country.

A good deal of this book has been birthed in the relationships and conversations which have taken place on and off the show since 1997. I have learned a great deal from my Catholic and Jewish friends about their faiths—but also about my own. I'm convinced that much of what we believe is clarified when we set it side-by-side with other faiths. I remember, for example, the first time Rabbi Federow told us the story of how he grew up in Springfield, Missouri under constant pressure by zealous Christian witnesses who urged him to accept Jesus as his Lord and Savior. As a conservative Jew, he developed a thick skin to withstand these "attacks." He also developed a series of arguments to counter Christian missionaries to the Jews point-by-point. As you can imagine, we've had some interesting and hard conversations on- and off-air about these issues. Our motto is, "We agree to disagree but don't become disagreeable." That has been true—most of the time. I recall a time when Father Frank Rossi, who taught moral theology at St. Mary's Seminary in Houston, talked about the nature of moral and immoral acts from the perspective of Catholic tradition. One evening, Father Michael Barrett, a priest of Opus Dei, offered our audience an amazing analysis from a Catholic perspective about the responsibilities of Christian businessmen and women to society and to God. One of the priests currently on the show, Father Mario Arroyo, is a philosophical theologian, and he consistently comes up with thoughtful responses to callers' questions and topics we discuss.

There have been other relationships and conversations which have also made their way onto the pages of this book one way or another. Because of my growing interest in interfaith dialogue, I have been in regular contact with some fine institutions and groups around the world: the Institute for Interfaith Dialogue in Houston, the Ahmaddiya Muslim community, and the Boniuk Institute for the Study and Advancement of Religious Tolerance at Rice University, to name a few. These institutions and their leaders have added a great deal to my knowledge and understanding about various peoples and their faiths. Dr. Jill Carroll, Dr. Carol Quillen, Dr. Muhammed Çetin, Dr. Alp Aslandogan, Dr. Amir Malik, Shahed Ahmed, Can Dogan, and Ali Candir have been patient with me as I stumbled into areas far outside my expertise. They have been good examples of what it means to be "slow to judge" and eager to listen. These women and men have added a great deal to my life, and I'm grateful for their kindness. If this book has strengths, they come from their collective wisdom. If it has weaknesses, they are my own.

I also want to acknowledge my appreciation to the good people at Thomas Nelson Publishers. Over the last decade, I have worked with Ecclesia Bible Society, Thomas Nelson, and more than one hundred others to create The Voice™ Bible (www.hearthevoice.com). It was my privilege to serve as the lead scholar and translator for the project. Over the last four years, I have served as the Thomas Nelson Research Professor at Houston Baptist University, a cooperative agreement between HBU and Thomas Nelson. Because of his love for the Scriptures and desire to extend the kingdom of God, my president, Dr. Robert Sloan, agreed to share some of my time and energies with Thomas Nelson for a season. Much of my attention has been given to talking with thousands of students, staff, and faculty at over forty universities and seminaries about the translation and about the changes taking place in society. While working with Thomas Nelson, many people have helped me—but two in particular have been with me throughout this entire project: Frank Couch and Maleah Bell. Over the last ten years, they have become dear friends and colleagues in our common cause and our love for the Scriptures. When Frank asked me to contribute a book to the new series *Refraction*, I was honored and pleased. It is my sincere prayer that readers will become people who are slow to judge and quick to listen, and that, by truly listening and learning from those who are different, we can all broaden and deepen our kingdom commitments.

Finally, I want to express my appreciation to my wife Cathy for her support while researching and writing this book. This project has taken me away from home and family when it would have been much more convenient for her, my sons, and my daughter-in-law for me to be present and attentive. But each of them contributed in their own way to help this book see the light of day. I can't tell you how fortunate and grateful I am to have their love and support.

David B. Capes
Thomas Nelson Research Professor
Houston Baptist University
Pentecost 2014

INTRODUCTION

People are quick to judge and slow to correct themselves.

—Ezio Auditore in *Assassin's Creed*[1]

In 2007, David Kinnaman, president of The Barna Group, and Gabe Lyons, founder of the Fermi project, published an important book entitled *unChristian: What a New Generation Really Thinks about Christianity . . . and Why It Matters*. The book is based on three years of research and analysis into the perception that "outsiders"—classified as Mosaics and Busters (16–29 year olds)—have of present-day Christianity. Both Kinnaman and Lyons began the project convinced that Christianity has an image problem. But after conducting thousands of surveys and interviews, they discovered that it wasn't just an image problem; it was a real problem in the heart and soul of modern Christianity. The negative perceptions were based largely on real attitudes and actions of Christian people which are downright "unChristian."

I want to share with you some of the impressions outsiders have of Christians. Now, you may disagree with these characterizations, but let me ask you to suspend judgment for a moment and listen to how people outside the faith view us. The first unfavorable image is this: 91 percent of outsiders consider Christians antihomosexual.[2] Is that true? Are Christians really antihomosexual? Whether it is true or not, that is the way it comes across. Here's another: 87 percent of outsiders regard Christians as "judgmental."[3] Now you may think calling a group of people "judgmental" is itself judgmental, but I ask you once again to listen, really listen, to what these folks think. They are saying something we need to hear. Another unflattering image that Christians need to consider is this: 85 percent of outsiders think Christians are hypocritical, and 78 percent of outsiders describe

Christians as old-fashioned.[4] This is ironic given the fact that Jesus and His first followers were on the cutting edge of society, reimagining the world redrawn around kingdom priorities. Seventy percent of non-Christians think Jesus followers are insensitive to other people. Closely related is this: 64 percent regard Christians as not accepting of other faiths.[5]

Note that "judgmental" ranked just below "antihomosexual" among the negative images of present-day Christianity. But when you think about it, judgmental attitudes and actions are responsible for the perceived—and often real—antihomosexual bias expressed by some Christians, as well as for insensitivity to others and not accepting of other faiths. It is important to note that the Christian church historically has held strong convictions about matters of sexuality—convictions which preclude certain kinds of sexual behaviors—but that does not have to translate into judgmental attitudes that stifle dialogue between gays and straights before the conversation even begins. Likewise, Christianity historically has set itself apart from other religions by its beliefs and practices—indeed, all religions do that—but that does not mean that Christians should act as if they are better than Muslims, Jews, Hindus, atheists, or others. The church today has more than an image problem; it has an attitude problem. That attitude turns judgmental too often and too quickly.

In this book, we hope to build on the excellent work of Kinnaman and Lyons. They have not only pointed out the problem; they have also offered some solutions to which we need to pay attention. Our approach is related and summarized well in the title of this book: *Slow to Judge: Sometimes It's OK to Listen.* Now, by saying "Slow to Judge," we are not suggesting that judgment, in and of itself, is morally wrong or out of order. Indeed, judgment should not always be viewed negatively. As we will see, God invites us to make right judgments and to help correct wrongs when we see them. So we might well create a slogan, "No judgment, no justice." In truth, we cannot develop vibrant, thriving communities if no one is able and willing to step in and offer timely correction. We cannot offer correction without exercising judgment. This is plainly illustrated when the apostle Paul reminded the Corinthians that, in the world to come, faithful men and women will be chosen by God to assist Him in ruling and judging the world:

> Don't you know that His people are destined to judge the world? If you have the authority to judge the world, can't you handle these small matters *and render a better judgment than the civil courts?* Further, don't you know that we are destined to judge the heavenly messengers? *So if we are to exercise authority in the heavenly realms,* can't we take care of the conflicts that arise in this life? (1 Cor. 6:2–3)

So Paul clearly thought that the people of God had a key role to play in the future in judging the nations. If they are to have this authority in the world to come, certainly they can begin to exercise that power in lesser matters now.

Now, if judging itself isn't the problem, what is? We tend to judge too quickly. In some cases, rather than doing the hard work demanded in order to judge justly, we prejudge the person or persons based on our own biases and superficial experiences. In other cases, we judge based on wrong or incomplete information. In both cases, we come to the wrong conclusion. I'm often amazed at the amount of time it takes lawyers, a judge, and a jury to prepare and try a case. Teams of lawyers spend months or years researching the matter (what really happened), carefully parsing any applicable laws, and deposing witnesses. At the trial, they pick a jury of the defendant's peers, make their arguments, and bring in the available witnesses. The lawyers plead their cases before a judge or a group of jurors. It often takes many weeks before juries reach a verdict. Even then, jury verdicts can be wrong, depending on what happened or didn't happen at the trial. My point is this: judging wisely and achieving justice is not easy, nor is it quick. It demands that we invest enough time and set aside our stereotypes about others in order to get it right. So this is why we've entitled the book *Slow to Judge*.

Another problem occurs when judgment (an action) becomes judgmental (an attitude). Often, judgmental attitudes are based on pride and the conviction that we (Christians) are right about everything, or at least most things.

THE PROBLEM OF PRIDE

Pride may well be the most subtle sin of our time, but it remains the deadliest. Pride sits just below the surface and raises its ugly head when we need it least. Compared to some of the more notorious and celebrated sins, pride is frequently viewed as a respectable transgression. A pastor may be dismissed for adultery, but never for pride alone. Stealing may land you in jail, but there is no felony conviction for a fit of arrogance. A Christian who is addicted to drugs or alcohol may be the talk of the town, but almost no one gossips over a person's addiction to hubris. Yet Scripture makes it clear that pride is one of the most hurtful flaws that a person may possess. Cornelius Plantinga writes that pride is "that blend of narcissism and conceit that we detest in others and sometimes tenderly protect in ourselves." He asks, "What sin . . . causes more wars, envies, fratricides, tyrannies, ethnic cleansings and general subversions of fellowship? What sin makes God seem more irrelevant?"[6] In truth, pride is the essence of all sorts of maladies affecting the human family, including our tendency to be judgmental. As C. S. Lewis noted, pride "is the complete anti-God state of mind."[7]

Pride's hurtful presence is manifested in a variety of ways. First, pride means that we are quick to find fault with other people while giving ourselves and our friends a pass. The Christian scriptures deal with this double standard and our tendency toward showing favoritism, as we will see later. Second, prideful people—regardless of their religious persuasion—like to hear themselves talk. They barely stop long enough to take a breath, much less to pause and truly analyze what other people actually think. And what do they talk about? Mostly themselves. They are self-absorbed. And you rarely hear them ask a genuine question to others. But when they do, you can watch the wheels turning in their head as they are preparing a response: a gotcha, a zinger, or "that's nothing, let me tell you about the time I . . . ." Another insidious way pride reveals itself is in the tendency to want to prove that they are right. In fact, being right and making sure that others know they are is more important to some than pointing people to God, who is the Right-Maker. In the end, the loneliest person in the room is often the fellow who has to be right all the time. Don't be that guy!

Our tendency to be quick to judge may be due to our silly, human pride, but Christians don't have the franchise on arrogance. Every person, regardless of their faith or lack thereof, struggles and fails the temptation test that pride sets before us. But Christians carry a large target on their backs these days for reasons we will discuss throughout the book.

As we saw earlier, the third most "unfavorable" image of Christianity these days is that it is hypocritical. But as my rabbi friend frequently points out, the charge that this or that group is hypocritical can be seen as a compliment. Sound strange? Perhaps. But think of it this way: we may fail to live up to our standards, but at least we have standards. And those who accuse Christians of being hypocrites recognize that Christianity has standards and values, even if some of its followers fail to live up to them. Furthermore, many of the standards Christians espouse are admired by outsiders. This is true of Christianity but also other religions. People, for example, may respect the family values of the Mormon faith, even as they disagree with its essential teachings. Likewise, there are elements in Judaism of discipline, generosity, and charity for the poor which most people admire. On the other hand, if a group of people aren't perceived as having standards and values, then they will never be subject to the charge that they are hypocrites. They may have standards, but outsiders have no clue what they are. So the charge that Christianity is hypocritical can be interpreted as a type of back-handed compliment.

But even if some Christians act hypocritically, not all do. Many people live out their faith day in and day out. You just never hear of them. If a televangelist falls from grace, then that is what people talk about. If hundreds of millions of Christians throughout the United States, Africa, Asia, South America, and Europe faithfully live by what their faith teaches, that is not considered newsworthy. There are, of course, high-profile Christians who have remained true to their values. It's hard to imagine a charge of hypocrisy being made against Mother Teresa or Dr. Billy Graham. I've never heard such a charge and dare say you haven't either. People may disagree with their politics, actions, or beliefs, but they will seldom criticize their morals.

Finally, just because people do not live up to the standards and values of the Christian faith does not mean the faith itself is at fault; the individuals are. A faith cannot be at fault if its followers fail to live up to its teachings. It is only when a faith teaches its followers to do evil, hurtful things that it can be charged with being evil. Our (mis)behavior may reflect badly on God, but that does not make God bad. I think this is the essence of that first petition of the Lord's prayer, "Hallowed be thy name" (Matt. 6:9 KJV). Many people take this as a statement of praise, "God, Your name is hallowed (or holy)." While that is certainly true, that is not the point in the prayer. "Hallowed be thy name" is not a declaration; it is a petition or a request. It would be better understood, "Father, keep Your name holy. Don't let us do anything that might give You a bad name or a black eye. Help us reflect well on You. Father, protect Your good name." So the charge that Christianity is hypocritical is a bit strange: individual Christians may be hypocritical, but the faith itself cannot be. Still, it would be nice if Christians were more committed to live by the faith they profess.

Let's move on from pride and hypocrisy to another concern. One of the leading reasons Christians are accused of being judgmental these days has to do with the state of faith in America and the West. Let's consider where we are these days.

MORALISTIC THERAPEUTIC DEISM

The charge that Christians are judgmental must be understood within our current, social context here in America and the West. Sociologists Christian Smith and Melinda Lundquist Denton, in their 2005 book *Soul Searching: The Religious and Spiritual Lives of American Teenagers*, have coined the phrase "Moralistic Therapeutic Deism" (abbreviated MTD) to describe the common religious beliefs held by most American teenagers. The book was the result of a study project funded by the Lilly Endowment. A team of researchers interviewed more than three thousand teenagers as part of the study. They identified five basic beliefs:

1. There is a god who created and ordered the world and watches over humanity.

2. This god wants us to be good, nice, and fair to each other, as most world religions teach.

3. The goal of life is to be happy and to feel good about ourselves.

4. This god only gets involved in our lives when we need him to solve a problem.

5. Good people go to heaven when they die.[8]

In this new American Religion, there are no creeds, no convictions, and no practices that define it. MTD has effectively infiltrated the American religious scene and reduced faith to morality and worship to therapy, all while insisting this god shows up only when we can't help ourselves. For many, this god is like Superman. He flies in to save the day just in the nick of time when Lois Lane is in real trouble and her life is on the line. But no sooner than he shows up, he's off again. MTD is a respectable religion to have if you are "spiritual but not religious." Except for perhaps secularism, MTD is vying to become the "civil religion" of the United States, a nation composed of many diverse populations. As a friend of mine says, "Houston is a city where there are over two hundred languages spoken every day before breakfast." That statement about one American city gives you a sense of how different we truly are. With all that difference around us, what are we to do?

Here is the problem: if MTD is our default religion here in America, anyone who claims more also demands more and insists on more than what MTD requires. That person could be accused of being fanatical, imposing his/her faith on others, or being judgmental. Kenda Creasy Dean, United Methodist minister and professor at Princeton Theological Seminary, writes, "The problem does not seem to be that churches are teaching young people badly, but that we are doing an exceedingly good job of teaching youth what we really believe: namely, that Christianity is not a big deal, that God requires little, and the church is a helpful social institution filled with nice people focused primarily on 'folks like us'—which, of course, begs the question of whether we are really the church at all."[9] According to Dean, pastors and parents have unwittingly passed on this watered-down mutation of Christianity. Why? Because we value safety and security over everything else; we are addicted to personal peace and affluence. Few are willing to risk their livelihood, their reputation, or their good name in a world where difference defines us. So MTD has become the ambient faith in America. It is a non-offensive, generic religion which is apparently in the air we breathe. When a Christ follower stands up to say, "This I believe . . . ," some are bound to be offended; others will accuse him or her of being insensitive, and still others will condemn him or her as judgmental. Ironic, isn't it?

Here in a nutshell is my thesis. It is possible to stand up for Jesus, to articulate your faith clearly as a witness, and to defend your faith effectively against opponents, while at the same time not being perceived as judgmental because you have been slow to judge and quick to listen. Now this will mean that there are times when you must sit back, suspend judgment, and truly listen as others defend their faiths and bear witness to you. You can't expect to be the only person heard in the conversation. And despite what you may think, this willingness to listen and take in what others have to say will not necessarily result in dumbing down or watering down your own commitments. In fact, I submit that, if you will set aside any judgmental impulse you have and dedicate yourself to understanding and listening to people very different from you, your own faith can and will grow stronger. As my rabbi friend Stuart Federow is fond of saying, "He who knows only one faith knows none." In other words, if all you know is Christianity, you probably don't have a good grasp of what you believe and why you believe it. It is when we juxtapose it with other faiths around us that we begin to see and understand the brilliance and uniqueness of our Christian faith.

I've seen the same dynamic in play many times in the teaching of languages. For more than twenty years, I have taught undergraduate and graduate students New Testament Greek at Houston Baptist University. After studying Greek for one year with me, most students will say, "You know, I have learned more about English and how my language works from your Greek class than I ever learned from all the grammar classes I took in high school and college." And it is true. When you learn that second language, you begin to understand how your own language works: what an infinitive does; what a participle does; or how case endings differ depending on the way a word is used. If you sit around and all you study is English, English, English, the chances are good that you will never know the difference between a participle and an infinitive or a compound and a complex sentence. The same dynamic is at work in other areas of knowledge like religion. If all we know is our faith and we never put it side-by-side with another, our own spiritual growth and commitments can be easily stunted.

A FRIEND OF SINNERS

One of the most consistent charges leveled against Jesus by His opponents was that He was a friend of sinners. When you read the Gospels, you realize how often Jesus was in the company of sinners. Now, I'm not using the word *sinners* in a generic sense, referring to everybody. We're all sinners. But the way it is frequently used in the Gospels is to refer to people whose lives were viewed by the vast majority as socially unacceptable. Jesus consistently befriended notorious sinners like tax collectors and prostitutes. He accepted their invitations to dinners and attended their parties. He appeared to enjoy their company more than the company of those who thought themselves "righteous."

Now let's be honest. Jesus was the sinless Son of God. He was God's Anointed, the Liberating King. If anyone could have been judgmental against such dishonorable people, it was Jesus. But He wasn't. Sinners made their way to Jesus, something they would not have done had He been judgmental. No, He welcomed sinners to the ranks of discipleship and predicted that they would enter God's kingdom before the self-described religious. Somehow—and this is what we need to work on—He called them to change their ways, but He did so without being judgmental. Jesus didn't leave "sinners" in their sin; He knew the kind of pain sin caused when it reigned unchecked in a life. Instead, He called them to a new life, a life of joy lived under the rule of God in the world. This account in Mark's Gospel (2:13–17) tells the story:

> [13]Another time Jesus was out walking alongside the Sea *of Galilee* teaching the gathering crowd as He went. [14]He saw Levi, the son of Alphaeus, sitting at the booth where he collected taxes.
>
> **JESUS** (*calling out to him*)**:** Follow Me.
>
> Levi left the booth and went along with Him.
>
> [15] At Levi's house, many tax collectors and other sinners—*Jews who did not keep the strict purity laws of the Jewish holy texts*— were dining with Jesus and His disciples. Jesus had attracted such a large following that all kinds of people surrounded Him. [16] When the Pharisees' scribes saw who shared the table with Jesus, they were quick to criticize:
>
> **SCRIBES** (*to His disciples*)**:** *If your master is such a righteous person,* then why does He eat and drink with tax collectors and sinners, *the worst among us?*

[17] Jesus heard them.

JESUS *(to the scribes)*: People who have their health don't need to see a doctor. Only those who are sick do. I'm not here to call those already in good standing with God; I'm here to call sinners to turn back to Him.

Jesus' invitation to follow Him, like His invitations to all the disciples, involves a lot more than joining the caravan. Jesus' invitation is for sinners to change their ways of life. Jesus makes it clear, despite the criticisms of some observers, that this invitation is indeed open to all—especially to the sinners who need it most. Jesus grants to those who choose Him not just companionship and forgiveness but the ability to truly receive a new identity and live a new life.[10]

When opponents pressed Jesus for why He enjoyed table fellowship with prostitutes and tax collectors, He was ready with an answer, "I came for these people." In a sense He was saying, "These are my kind of people." Why? They were poor in spirit (Matt. 5:3), and they knew it. They weren't putting on airs. They didn't think they were something they weren't. They realized that their spiritual bank account had a zero balance. They understood that they were not well and needed a physician. Jesus was just such a healer.

David Kinnaman and Gabe Lyons discovered a common theme in their research, "Christians often err on the side of being quick to judge others, even fellow believers, feeling as though they know the answers, as though they know what God must think."[11] I'm afraid this disposition is so deeply ingrained in us and our culture that it's going to be hard to root out and overcome; but it is necessary to do so if we are to bear witness to the God who is loving, patient, slow to anger, slow to judge, and quick to listen.

After interviewing people outside the faith, Kinnaman and Lyons make a number of recommendations on how to develop an atmosphere of mutual respect between Christians and non-Christians. I've adapted these to my own purposes here:

1. Listen more, talk less. You may learn something important.

2. Don't label other people or try to fit them into nice, neat little boxes.

3. Don't pretend you have all the answers. Be willing to say, "I don't know."

4. Put yourself in the other's place. Or as the saying goes, "Walk a mile in my shoes."

5. Be authentic. Recognize when you are trying to push your agenda on others.

6. Be a true friend with no other motives. Friendship has its rewards. Don't make people your special project.[12]

Notice how many of these recommendations have to do with listening to others and holding off on judging them. Our own approach will build on these and yet go further. We will take as our marching orders some key passages of Scripture. Let's set these out at the beginning.

James 1:19–20	"Listen, open your ears, harness your desire to speak, and don't get worked up into a rage so easily, my brothers and sisters. Human anger *is a futile exercise that* will never produce God's kind of justice *in this world.*"
Colossians 3:12–14	"Since you are all set apart by God, made holy and dearly loved, clothe yourselves with *a holy way of life:* compassion, kindness, humility, gentleness, and patience. Put up with one another. Forgive. Pardon any offenses against one another, as the Lord has pardoned you, because you should act in kind. But above all these, put on love! Love is the perfect tie to bind these together."
John 7:24	"You should not judge by outward appearance. When you judge, search for what is right and just."
Luke 6:31	"Think of the kindness you wish others would show you; do the same for them."

Taken together, these verses provide an overview of the kind of approach that I plan to take in this book. If we are to be slow to judge and quick to listen, then we are going to need to tap into some of these spiritual resources. I don't think it wise to bring these teachings down into a list of propositions, a list of things to do; instead, we want to step into the story of Scripture so we can align our lives to God's purposes.

Over the next few chapters, you will be given some stories from Scripture and from culture. Some will be familiar. Some will be new. In a few cases, familiar stories will seem new because of the way they are told. The goal is to help us envision ourselves as faithful witnesses to God who are nevertheless willing to listen to people with drastically different stories. In those exchanges, when we suspend judgment and truly listen, we are going to find truth and beauty and goodness in some of the most unexpected places. We will also find that, if we truly listen, we may be given a chance to speak.

With James let us pray that the Lord will open our ears so we may truly listen.

A LISTENING HEART

"Please give Your servant a listening heart for judging Your people and for knowing the difference between what is good and what is evil."

—King Solomon (1 Kings 3:9)

"Whenever it shows up, we expect wisdom may have a face."

—Mark McMinn[1]

ike many, I've stumbled into some of the best things of life. Without really meaning to or planning it, I've found friendships and connections that have profoundly influenced and shaped my life. How did this Georgia boy who grew up Baptist end up with a conservative rabbi and Catholic priest as two of his best and most enduring friends? It wasn't planned; it just happened. Providence, you say? I agree.

I didn't start life with an interest in interfaith or intercultural dialogue. It just sort of happened. I didn't have a deep desire to study other religions formally or informally, but I did take an occasional course in world religions along the way, the kind offered by most colleges and universities. Still, engaging people of different faiths, backgrounds, and cultures has become a weekly—if not daily—part of my life. On more than one occasion, those experiences have meant that I have had to be slow to judge and quick to listen.

Now, before we go any further, let me relate to you a story from the Bible that ought to set the table nicely. If you've read the Bible, you are probably familiar with this account. If not, then this may be brand new. Still, even if you have read the story, I'll bet there is a detail or two in it that you have never noticed because—to be honest—most English translations don't make it that easy. Let me tell the story and then get down to some precise language in one of the verses.

Solomon had become king. He had been anointed by God's prophet, indicating God's choice for who would lead His people. Then he had been acclaimed by the people, demonstrating that he was the people's choice to rule over them. Many years earlier, David's court prophet Nathan had said this day would come. Saul's dynasty had not lasted—in fact, he was a one-king dynasty—but God promised David that his son would sit on the throne of Israel and would build Him a temple (2 Sam. 7:12–16). So when King David breathed his last, he had confidence that his son Solomon would inherit a united and strong Israel. There were challenges that had to be met for the young king to consolidate power; but once those challenges were behind him, Solomon had a chance to sit back and think seriously about the future. What kind of king would he be? How would he make the tough decisions that kings and other rulers are always called to make? What kind of leaders would he choose to advise him? How would he lead the people in a time of war? How would he deal with his own people when they opposed him? Although Solomon had already received a royal education, he knew he needed more. Solomon needed wisdom.

> **Although Solomon had already received a royal education, he knew he needed more. Solomon needed wisdom.**

One night, the Eternal God came to the king in a dream and invited him to make a single request (1 Kings 3:5). Wisely, Solomon didn't just blurt out the first thing that popped into his mind. He began by rehearsing all the ways God had been faithful to his father David, and how David had remained faithful to God. For a time, he contemplated God's loyal love, especially when He allowed David's own son to sit on the throne of Israel. But Solomon knew he was young and inexperienced. He knew, too, the immensity of the task ahead. To lead a nation so young and vulnerable to its enemies, to shepherd a flock so large and diverse—how was he to do it? So, Solomon made his simple request: "Please give Your servant a listening heart for judging Your people and for knowing the difference between what is good and what is evil. Who is capable of judging Your *chosen* ones, a great people?" (1 Kings 3:9).

So what exactly did Solomon ask for? He asked for "a listening heart," a heart that *truly* listens, not *seems to* listen, not pretends to listen while trying to figure out how to reply or how to get one up on an opponent. Solomon had watched his father well. He knew that being king meant making hard decisions and passing judgment, not just on big things but on little things, as well. He knew he needed "a listening heart" to pull it off. He knew he needed "a listening heart" to be a great king.

Other translations have rendered the same phrase a bit differently:

an understanding mind (ESV, NRSV)

a discerning heart (NIV)

an understanding heart (NKJV)

Now, all these are legitimate and helpful renderings of the Hebrew, but I prefer the more literal translation of "a listening heart" because it reflects the profound need we have to speak and be heard. Today there is no lack of speaking—everyone is speaking, blogging, writing, and clamoring to be heard—but how many are listening? I mean, *truly* listening? I heard a funny line about blogging once, "Never have so many said so little to so few." The point is that everybody's talking but few are listening. In order to judge well, understand well, and discern right from wrong, you must start with a listening heart.

> To be wise, one must learn to listen, and the best place to begin listening is to the wisdom of the ages.

The king's wise request pleased God. Most people would have asked for a long, healthy life or great personal fortune or honor in battle. Instead, Solomon asked for the ability to understand his people and be able to administer justice, one of the main things a king had to do in those days. So God granted his request and gave him the ability to hear and to know what is right. In a word, God gave Solomon "wisdom."

This is why Solomon's name has become so closely associated with wisdom. According to tradition, the good king authored, collected, and inspired the composition of many proverbs. We will consider a few of these in this book because, to be wise, one must learn to listen, and the best place to begin listening is to the wisdom of the ages recorded in Holy Scripture. Tradition credits Solomon with writing two of the most significant wisdom books in the Old Testament: Ecclesiastes and Song of Solomon. But perhaps most significantly for our purposes, many of the proverbs are known broadly as the proverbs of Solomon. Moreover, Israel's wise king inspired the poets and singers of Israel to compose wisdom psalms, such as Psalms 1 and 14.

We will define *wisdom* from the Bible's point of view—but first, let's consider five things that wisdom is *not*.

1. Wisdom is not automatic. No one gets wisdom routinely. You aren't just born with it. There is no "Wisdom DNA." It is not the result of some natural process. Wisdom must be cultivated like a garden. Everyone may have the capacity for wisdom, but not everyone develops it. Even Solomon, in all his glory, had to cultivate wisdom, seek it out, and make it his own.

2. Wisdom is not raw intelligence. Some people are gifted with raw intelligence. They have unusual academic abilities and can excel in their studies if they put their minds to it. But wisdom is not equated with raw intelligence or innate smartness. Many intelligent people end up making foolish decisions and living badly.

3. Wisdom also has nothing to do with education. A person may have a PhD in any number of subjects and still be a fool, from the biblical perspective. Education is the acquisition of skills, competencies, and knowledge, but at a very basic level that has nothing to do with wisdom. Recently, I was talking with a psychology professor who was telling me that doctors—some of the most educated people in society—have one of the highest rates of successful suicides. The acquisition of knowledge often takes place apart from wisdom.

4. Wisdom is not the result of hard knocks. We should not equate it with "street smarts." Now sometimes, people who endure a life of hardship develop wisdom, but there are no guarantees. There is no direct cause-and-effect

relationship between suffering and wisdom. More often than not, people who experience life's hard stuff turn out to be bitter and angry. No one would describe them as wise.

5. Wisdom is not the result of growing old. Let's consider the well-known American proverb, "There's no fool like an old fool." Age may temper us and in ways make us calmer and better; it may smooth off the rough edges. But none of that is guaranteed. Everyone has met older people who are harsh, opinionated, unkind, and impatient. The term "old codger" comes to mind. Many old people are not wise at all. In order to be wise, growing old must be combined with something else.

Well, then, what is wisdom, biblically speaking? Let me give a brief—and what I hope will be helpful—definition, and you will see how it relates to King Solomon and the concerns of this book.

Wisdom is the ability to live life well and make good decisions.

That's it. It's so simple most people stumble over it. But think about it for a moment. Wouldn't it be wonderful if we could live life well? Wouldn't it be magnificent to look back over our lives and say we have lived well and made the right decisions? We married the right person (though it may be wise for many to remain single). We chose the right vocation. We went to the right schools. We spent our time and money wisely. We had good and lasting friendships with the people who made us better. We enjoyed relatively good health because we feasted well, fasted often, and rested enough. Wisdom is that ability to live well, and it comes, according to Solomon, by developing a listening heart and truly listening to wise people like our parents, our mentors, our friends, our spiritual leaders, our employers, our neighbors in need, and sometimes even people who are very different from us.

Now, notice a key to what Solomon says about wisdom and knowledge, "The worship of the Eternal One, *the one True God,* is the first step toward knowledge" (Prov. 1:7). Knowledge in the poetry of Proverbs is a synonym for wisdom. The mechanism for developing wisdom and knowledge is this, "a listening heart." But the first step in that direction is to know the one True God and stand in respect and awe of Him. Worship is our appropriate response to knowing who God is and knowing who we are in relation to Him. Trouble comes and fools rush in when we imagine we are more than we are—stronger than we are, smarter than we are, more impor- tant than we are—and when we dare to think that we as creatures can somehow get on without our Creator.

Fast-forward to the New Testament letter of James. This little book in the back of the Bible is widely understood to be the most thoroughgoing example of early Christian wisdom. Here are a few key verses from the opening chapter:

> If any of you lacks wisdom, let him ask of God, who gives to all liberally and without reproach, and it will be given to him. But let him ask in faith, with no doubting, for he who doubts is like a wave of the sea driven and tossed by the wind. For let not that man suppose that he will receive anything from the Lord; he is a double-minded man, unstable in all his ways. (James 1:5–8 NKJV)

What does James add to the mix? Simply this: wisdom is God's gift to those who ask. Again, wisdom is not a natural by-product of just living; it comes to us as God's gift when we pause long enough to ask sincerely for it. Notice, too, that we have to be wise enough in the first place to know that we lack wisdom. Some unfortunately don't ever get that far. God gives, James says, "liberally and without reproach"—in other words, "He gives lavishly and never scolds you for asking" (James 1:5).

When we ask for wisdom, James teaches, we must ask in faith. Faith in this instance means trust; it is a sense of absolute dependency on God. As a poker-playing friend of mine says, "Faith is the decision to go 'all in' with God." Some translations, I'm afraid, miss the point when they render the Greek original "ask in faith, with no doubting," as if doubt is the opposite of faith.

Let me suggest something that may strike you as a bit radical: doubt is not the opposite of faith. People of great faith often struggle with doubts. Consider how often the biblical psalms question God and dabble in "doubt." Recall how Mother Teresa—one of the greatest saints of the twentieth century—struggled at times with intellectual questions and doubt. Most men and women of great faith I have known have worked through doubts at key moments in their spiritual journeys. In fact, doubts may be important signposts along the journey of a life well lived. The opposite of faith is not doubt; it is willful disbelief. In fact, the word often translated "doubt" here in James 1:5–8 means to make a decision on your own without reference to God. It is the opposite of the counsel found in Proverbs.

> Trust in the LORD with all your heart,
> And lean not on your own understanding;
> In all your ways acknowledge Him,
> And He shall direct your paths. (Prov. 3:5–6 NKJV)

James, I believe, was inspired by Proverbs 3 when he reflected on wisdom. Ask in faith and do not lean on your own understanding. Leaning on your own understanding is the opposite of faith; it is contrary to trusting in the Lord with all your heart. If we say to God, "God, I've got this one," or "God, I'll take it from here," we aren't doubting God's existence or His good name or His power to help us; what we are doing is taking the wheel and telling God to take the back seat. That's not wisdom, that's foolishness. It's as if we say, "God, You take care of the big stuff—like healing my diseases and getting me to heaven when I die—but I'll take care of the little stuff" (secretly knowing that much of life is made up of the little stuff). James's point is this: when we ask for wisdom from God, we must not fall back into trusting—or preferring—our own finite, flawed knowledge. Once we launch the ship of faith, once we leave the shore, we don't look back or choose to take the helm in our own hand.

The apostle Paul addresses wisdom, but he adds an interesting twist that we must not miss:

> Look carefully at your call, brothers and sisters. By human standards, not many of you are deemed to be wise. Not many are considered powerful. Not many of you come from royalty, right? But *celebrate this*: God selected the world's foolish to bring shame upon *those who think they are* wise; likewise, He selected the world's weak to bring disgrace upon *those who think they are* strong. God selected the common and the castoff, whatever lacks status, so He could invalidate the claims of those who think those things are significant. So it makes no sense for any person to boast in God's presence. Instead, credit God with your new situation: you are united with Jesus the Anointed. He is God's wisdom for us and more. He is our righteousness and holiness and redemption. As the Scripture says: "If someone wants to boast, he should boast in the Lord." (I Cor. 1:26–31)

When all is said and done, Paul makes a profound point that we must not fail to notice. Ultimately, wisdom is not a *what*; it is a *Who*. Jesus, the Messiah, is God's wisdom for us. Though we may not have expected it, wisdom has a face. Jesus embodies the totality of God's wisdom. As Jesus walked the earth, He was a sage who dispensed heaven's wisdom to His disciples and any who would truly listen.

Now, He has sent the Holy Spirit as our *Paraclete*, the One who is called to our side, the advocate who is to guide us into all wisdom and remind us of Jesus' words and ways. Ultimately, our pursuit of wisdom will lead us to a person: Jesus of Nazareth. As He lives in us and as we abide in Him, we move closer to experiencing God's wisdom in our lives.

But before we leave Paul, let's also notice something else he said. There is a quality which this world calls wisdom that is not wisdom at all; it is more akin to foolishness. Oh, on a popular level, it is honored as wisdom, treated as wisdom, celebrated as wisdom, but in the end the world's bogus wisdom will not lead to good decisions, a good life, or a good society. This worldly wisdom looks down on God's chosen ones and deems them fools. But radically and subversively, God is on the move undermining everything the worldly wise hold dear and significant. God selects the poor and weak, the marginalized, and the castoffs to demonstrate the ultimate bankruptcy of the world's wisdom. And it all began with the cross:

> For people who are stumbling toward ruin, the message of the cross is nothing but a tall tale for fools by a fool. But for those of us who are already experiencing the reality of being rescued *and made right*, it is nothing short of God's power. This is why the Scripture says:
>
>> I will put an end to the wisdom of the *so-called* wise,
>>> and I will invalidate the insight of your *so-called* experts.
>
> *So now,* where is the philosopher? Where is the scholar? Where is the skilled debater, the best of your time? *Step up, if you dare.* Hasn't God made fools out of *those who count on* the wisdom of this *rebellious, broken* world? For in God's *deep* wisdom, *He made it so that* the world could not even begin to comprehend Him through its own style of wisdom; in fact, God

took immense pleasure in rescuing people of faith through the foolishness of the message we preach. It seems the Jews are always asking for signs and the Greeks are always on the prowl for wisdom. *But we tell a different story.* We proclaim a crucified Jesus, God's Anointed. For Jews this is scandalous, for outsiders this is moronic, but for those of us living out God's call—regardless of our Jewish or Greek heritage—we know the Anointed embodies God's *dynamic* power and God's *deep* wisdom. *You can count on this:* God's foolishness will always be wiser than mere human wisdom, and God's weakness will always be stronger than mere human strength. (1 Cor. 1:18–25)

The message of the cross has a deeply polarizing power. Those stumbling toward ruin are quick to pass judgment on it and deem it foolish tales, pure and simple. But those who have a sense that God is rescuing them and making all things right find immense power in the cross. In short, in this new era of salvation, God is turning the world upside down. A great reversal is taking place. The high and mighty are brought low. The humble and weak are exalted. The crucified Messiah may offend some and seem moronic to others, but those who experience His liberation find dynamic power and deep wisdom in God's Anointed.

James, the brother of the Lord, offers his own commentary on the world's wisdom:

The wisdom of this world should never be mistaken for heavenly wisdom; it originates below in the earthly realms, with the demons. Any place where you find jealousy and selfish ambition, you will discover chaos and evil thriving under its rule. Heavenly wisdom centers on purity, peace, gentleness, deference, mercy, and other good fruits untainted by hypocrisy. The seed that flowers into righteousness will always be planted in peace by those who embrace peace. (James 3:15–18)

The wisdom from below has devilish origins, James says, and it coddles jealousy and selfish ambition. If the world's bogus wisdom wins the day, then chaos and evil will be the prevailing winds. A good life and good society will be only a distant hope. Heavenly wisdom, however, will lead us together to good lives founded on excellent decisions. It will baptize our broken world in qualities we long to see: purity, peace, gentleness, deference, and mercy.

This book is all about wisdom, defined in personal terms as the ability to live life well and make good decisions; but given our topic, we must expand this definition in social terms. If enough people live according to heaven's wisdom, we'll find ourselves living in good societies despite the differences that often divide us. Our purpose, then, is to explore key aspects of that wisdom—specifically, the wisdom of developing a listening heart, being slow to judge and quick to listen. But in order to recognize what we could become beneath God's wise wings, we must consider the reality in which we find ourselves today. Unfortunately, worldly wisdom encourages us to make snap judgments, categorize people and their ideas so that we can easily dismiss them, and be quick to speak over them so no one has a chance to hear what they have to say. Ironically, many modern people behave this way even as they claim to be the most sensitive, most sympathetic, and most tolerant people. But these claims made by the world's bogus wisdom ring hollow, since it always despises a listening heart and pokes fun at every attempt to truly hear and respect others.

So here is what you can expect. This book will rub across the grain. It will rub across the grain of a world that is reluctant to start where true wisdom begins: the fear of the Eternal. It will rub across

> **The wisdom from below has devilish origins . . . and it coddles jealousy and selfish ambition.**

the grain of those schooled to jump to conclusions and rush to judgment. It will rub across the grain of everyone who is unwilling to consider the audacious claims of Jesus, God's wisdom for us. Perhaps it will rub across your grain, too, if you have been groomed too long to accept the world's bogus wisdom. Still, by the end of these chapters, you will be ready to engage people more authentically, be less prone to judge, and discover that sometimes it is best to listen.

With Solomon let us pray that God will grant us a listening heart.

QUESTIONS TO CONSIDER

1. Imagine yourself in Solomon's place: God has just made you the ruler over your entire homeland—and He has said to you, "Tell Me, what is your request of Me?" (1 Kings 3:5). What do you ask Him for?

2. In the previous question, did you list "listening heart" as something you'd ask God for? In your own words, what is a listening heart? What does it look like in day-to-day experience?

3. Read James 1:5–8. What conditions does God require of a person if he is to receive wisdom? What does it mean to be "dizzy and confused" (v. 8) or a "double-minded man" (NKJV)? What causes this? What is the solution?

4. Worship is our appropriate response to knowing who God is and knowing who we are in relation to Him. Spend some time right now in worship of God.

"DO NOT JUDGE" . . . REALLY?

2

If you've been around Christians very long, you're likely to have heard someone say, "You shouldn't judge. After all, Jesus said, 'Judge not, that ye be not judged'" (Matt. 7:1 KJV). For some reason, they always quote the King James Version on this. Apparently, they think Jesus must have prohibited His followers from ever forming or expressing any kind of judgment on anyone. That's kind of a strange conclusion given the fact that Jesus Himself goes on to make judgments and express them in the next few verses, "Don't give precious things to dogs. Don't cast your pearls before swine. If you do, the pigs will trample the pearls with their *little pigs'* feet, and then they will turn back and attack you" (Matt. 7:6). Jesus is not talking about farm animals here. He is categorizing some people very negatively in order to warn His disciples not to persist in sharing the gospel of the kingdom with those who reject it.

The language is about as derogatory as you find in the New Testament. Dogs here are not the cute, fuzzy puppies we take into our homes as pets, but packs of roaming hounds that menace the streets where children play and the elderly stroll. And in a Jewish context, swine are unclean animals to be avoided at all costs. Some people, according to Jesus, are like dogs; others are like swine. You have to be careful what good things you place before them. Jesus has formed an opinion. Jesus has expressed it. Jesus has judged.

Later in the same chapter, Jesus warns His disciples, "Along the way, watch out for false prophets. They will come to you in sheep's clothing, but underneath *that quaint and innocent wool,* they are hungry wolves. But you will recognize them by their fruits" (Matt. 7:15–16). Jesus pronounces "Woe" on the teachers of the law and the Pharisees, frequently calling them hypocrites, blind guides, white-washed graves: "Woe to you Pharisees, woe to you who teach the law, hypocrites! You traverse hills and mountains and seas to make one convert, and then when he does convert, you make him much more a son of hell than you are" (Matt. 23:15). The point is that Jesus makes judgments about people—some of which are very negative—and expresses them freely. So whatever "judge not" means, it can't mean "don't form an opinion" or "don't express it." Jesus surely did.

> **Jesus makes judgments about people— some of which are very negative— and expresses them freely.**

I can hear someone say, "Well, He's Jesus. He can do that sort of thing. But we shouldn't; we're not Jesus." True, we're not Jesus; but we are told to follow Jesus, to be like Him and imitate His life. If Jesus made judgments about others and warned others about them, then we should too. Indeed, if we don't discern between good fruit and bad fruit (another metaphor), then we put ourselves and our communities at risk.

So what did Jesus mean? In order to understand the context, let's look at the entire passage, rather than isolate a single verse. Here is how The Voice translates Matthew 7:1–5:

> **JESUS:** If you judge *other people,* then you will find that you, too, are being judged. ² Indeed, you will be judged by the

very standards to which you hold other people. [3] Why is it that you see the dust in your brother's or sister's eye, but you can't see what is in your own eye? [4] Don't ignore the wooden plank in your eye, while you criticize the speck of sawdust in your brother's eyelashes. [5] That type of criticism and judgment is a sham! Remove the plank from your own eye, and then perhaps you will be able to see clearly how to help your brother flush out his sawdust.

When you take Matthew 7:1 in isolation, you think you are dealing with a directive, "Don't judge!" But in fact, when you read it in context, you realize that Jesus is talking about something quite different and important. He is showing His disciples how they ought to go about correcting a brother or a sister. Let me explain.

Jesus is a sage, the embodiment of divine wisdom, and He teaches using various forms like parables, beatitudes, and commentaries on Scripture. On occasion, He also teaches in a particular style using a wisdom formula that has four parts: (1) admonition; (2) rationale; (3) illustration (in this case, a humorous one at that); (4) restatement and clarification of the original admonition. The structure made it easy to remember and pass on to others. So the entire passage (7:1–5) must be read together in order to make sense. To isolate one part from the other is to violate the true meaning of the text. As a friend of mine says, "Every text without a context is a pretext."

So let's take this in all four parts:

Admonition: Be careful how you judge your brother or sister.

Rationale: You will be judged in the same way (by God).

Illustration: The speck in your neighbor's eye/the wooden plank in your own

Restatement: Remove the plank from your own eye so you can see well enough to remove the speck from your neighbor's eye.

The point of Jesus' wise saying is to instruct Christ followers on how to go about correcting one another; He is not forbidding judgment. Now, before you think this could apply to anyone needing correction, notice this: Jesus' repeated use of "brother" implies that He is referring primarily to what happens in Christian community. It has nothing to do with how we are to approach secular society or our non-Christian friends. Jesus' teaching has to do only with how believers are to relate to one another in those awkward yet neces-sary moments when correction inside the community is essential.

The assumption is that the church will need correction from time to time and ought to be a self-correcting body. We shouldn't ask for outsiders to point out our hypocrisies and flaws. We shouldn't invite the government to come in and sort things out when things go awry. We shouldn't wait for the media to get wind of a problem and shout it from the rooftops. We are to help each other discover our flaws and seek to remove them. The question is: How do we go about it? Do we do it in harsh tones, going around acting all judgmental about others? Do we put on our holier-than-thou clothes and seek out sinners among our ranks? Do we set up fault-finding committees to roam about town under the guise of keeping the church pure? I would hope not.

The prerequisite for judging another is humility.

What is clear from Jesus' teaching is this: the prerequisite for judging another is humility. Without humility and without inspecting our own faults first, we should best remain silent. Beyond that, it is also obvious that unfair and unloving judgments are to be avoided at all costs. As we learned earlier, one of the things outsiders often say about Christians is that they are way too judgmental and act as if they are better than others. Apparently, we haven't been listening to Jesus. His wisdom statement here doesn't leave room for that. Before you seek to help a brother or sister correct their tiny flaw, you must examine yourself first to see whether you have some huge, obvious flaw that might keep you from seeing correctly. The contrast between the speck and the plank is almost comical: before you address the tiny, insignificant flaw in a fellow believer, make sure you don't have some gross failure hanging over your head. Only after you have dealt with your problem are you in a place to help others deal with theirs. This kind of correction can't happen at the drop of the hat; it can't happen automatically. If it must happen, it must happen slowly.

PAUL'S TROUBLED CHILD

If you have enough children, one of them is bound to break your heart. Paul, the Lord's emissary, had started a lot of churches and had a lot of spiritual children out there; the church that caused him the most grief was the one in Corinth. That's why it got so much of his attention. Although we have only two of his letters to Corinth, we know he wrote at least four, maybe more. Take a look at what he said in one of them (1 Cor. 6:1–7):

> [1]*Here's another troubling issue.* If you have a grievance against another *follower of Jesus*, do you have the audacity to bring that brother or sister into the civil courts rather than submitting yourselves to the authority of God's people? [2]Don't you know that His people are destined to judge the world? If you have the authority to judge the world, can't you handle these small matters *and render a better judgment than the civil courts*? [3]Further, don't you know that we are destined to judge the heavenly messengers? *So if we are to exercise authority in the heavenly realms,*

can't we take care of the conflicts that arise in this life? ⁴ To put it another way, if you are asking the courts to adjudicate your mundane conflicts, aren't you placing your problems under the authority of judges who have no standing within the church? ⁵ My words should embarrass you. Is it possible that you have no one among you with the wisdom to mediate between two siblings? ⁶ So one brother sues another brother *in public and drags the dispute* before outsiders who have no allegiance to Jesus?

⁷ The truth is that these *public* lawsuits cause all of you to lose and lose big. Wouldn't it be better to be ripped off or defrauded?

Apparently, Paul had gotten wind that some in Corinth couldn't settle their differences so they were taking their cases to the civil courts. Their spiritual father couldn't believe that they'd air their dirty laundry in public. It discredits the church and calls into question their claim that God can reconcile all things through Jesus. He clearly thinks the church ought to step in and help settle these disputes among brothers and sisters in Christ. The church in Corinth, despite its many problems, has the Holy Spirit, and it possesses enough collective wisdom to sort these things out if people will just submit to their leaders. After all, God's people are destined to judge the world and to judge heaven's messengers. When Christians take their problems into the public, God gets a black eye. Paul even suggests that they should be willing to be defrauded before they resort to the courts.

The point is that Paul understands that situations arise in which believers need correction. It's for the good of those directly involved and the good of the church to seek out some sort of local mediation. Relationships depend on it. This requires the people of God to exercise careful judgment. So Paul would not have read Jesus'

statement as an absolute prohibition, "Thou shalt not judge . . . ever."
It's *how* you judge that is important.

Rather than seeing Jesus' directive here as a prohibition against
any form of judgment, we need to hear it for what it really is:
guidance on how to deal with the inevitable issues that arise in
relationships.

In the art of biblical interpretation, there is a principle: let
Scripture interpret Scripture. Often the best explanation of a difficult passage in the Bible is another passage which is a bit clearer.
Paul provides us with a helpful bit of instruction in his letter to the
churches of Galatia (Gal. 6:1–5):

> ¹My spiritual brothers and sisters, if one *of our faithful* has fallen
> into a trap and is snared by sin, *don't stand idle and watch his
> demise.* Gently restore him, being careful not to step into your
> own snare. ²Shoulder each other's burdens, and then you will
> live as the law of the Anointed teaches us. ³Don't *take this
> opportunity to* think you are better than those who slip because
> you aren't; then you *become the fool and* deceive even yourself.
> ⁴Examine your own works so that if you are proud, it will be
> because of your own accomplishments and not someone else's.
> ⁵Each person has his or her own burden to bear *and story to
> write.*

The Galatian churches, like the Corinthian church, were plagued
with problems, but their worries seemed to come from outsiders
who had arrived after Paul had moved on to start other churches.
Apparently, troublemakers were trying to alter the Galatians' understanding of the gospel in ways that Paul felt undermined his credibility and ultimately put the whole church in jeopardy.

The emissary of Christ may well be thinking of Jesus' teaching
in the Sermon on the Mount when he writes these words. He
recognizes that there will be times when Christ-followers fall into

sin and need correction. He has just listed a series of vices which
entice the flesh: corrupt sexual relationships, impurity, unbridled lust,
idolatry, witchcraft, hatred, arguments, jealousy, anger, selfishness,
contentiousness, divisions, envy of other people's good fortunes,
drunkenness, and the like (Gal. 5:19–21). Perhaps he has these kinds
of flesh-traps in mind. But for Paul, sin is not just a deliberate act of
the will to disobey God and step across a reasonable boundary. Oh,
it is that. But it also manifests itself at times as a power at work in
us, causing us to act in ways we deplore. Elsewhere, Paul talks about
what it means to be a slave to sin (Rom. 6–8). That's why he can
speak here of a faithful person being trapped by sin. Sin has him and
won't let him go.

So what is the church to do in a situation when one of its own
is ensnared by sin? What must not happen is for his brothers or
sisters to look the other way or sweep it under the rug or hope he
works it out on his own. What must not happen is for the transgression to become public knowledge outside the community so as to
discredit the church and God. No, when the spiritual see a person
who has fallen and needs to be restored, they are to help put him
back together again *gently*, not harshly, and certainly not judgmentally
as if they have it all together. Again, humility is a prerequisite to the
gentleness needed to assist a fallen brother or sister. But like Jesus,
Paul urges the would-be restorers to consider first their own snares
and entanglements (the wooden planks in their own eyes). They
must never forget how vulnerable they are to the same or similar
temptations. Furthermore, they must never imagine for one second
that they could not be entrapped in a more insidious sin—namely,
the sin of pride that says, "That could never happen to me." It is easy
for those not trapped in a particular sin to condemn another for the
misstep. It is hard to put yourself in their place regarding the kind of
flesh-trap that typically overwhelms them.

It's significant, I think, that Paul urges the spiritual brothers and sisters (plural) to assist the fallen and restore him. Apparently, the apostle didn't think the job of restoration to be a solo task; he expected that it would take a team of faithful, spiritual men or women to work together to restore their sin-snared neighbor. After reading Dietrich Bonhoeffer's book *Life Together*[1] many years ago, I've had a sense that it is important to limit the circle of those in the know about the failings of a brother or sister. There is no need to broadcast it widely; it can do more damage than good to the church and to the individual. But the circle has to be wide enough to include the kind of people who are sufficiently wise, gentle, and spiritual to be able to address the snare and bring about full and complete restoration for the fallen.

Interestingly, Paul seems to take the teaching a bit further—or at least he attempts to work out the community's role in what it could mean to step in to restore a prodigal brother or sister. If we take Paul's instructions here seriously, it means that we must be willing to help them shoulder the burdens they are carrying as a result of their sins. It's not enough to point out a wrong and say, "Fix it, and remember, we'll be watching." Instead, we must be willing to say, "In order to fix this, we're willing to help you clean up the mess." And not just say it, but do it. This requires a radical commitment to reconciliation and forgiveness, neither of which come cheap. Bearing one another's burdens, Paul says, is the fulfillment of "the law of Christ" (Gal. 6:2 NKJV), a law written not in stone but founded on the example Jesus left us and grounded in the command to love one another. As Paul wrote earlier, "For the whole law comes down to this one instruction: 'Love your neighbor as yourself'" (Gal. 5:14, quoting Lev. 19:18).

> **It's not enough to point out a wrong and say, "Fix it, and remember, we'll be watching."**

Will Willimon is one of my favorite writers. In his book *What's Right with the Church*, he relates a story that I think illustrates perfectly what Jesus and Paul were talking about. It has to do with a conversation that took place among a group of area ministers over coffee.

> One of the ministers said that he thought that abortion was immoral.
>
> "Do you mean that you would ask a thirteen-year-old girl who got pregnant, God knows how, to raise a child by herself? Do you think that a thirteen year old is capable of being a mother?" one of his colleagues said . . . .
>
> "Well, no," replied the antiabortionist. "I suppose there would be some extreme circumstances in which abortion would be justified."
>
> "So what's wrong with a thirteen year old having a baby?" asked another minister. He was a black minister, a pastor of a large black congregation in town. "We have young girls who have this happen to them. I have a fourteen year old in my congregation who had a baby last month. We're going to baptize the child next Sunday," he added.
>
> "Do you really think that she is capable of raising a little baby?" another minister asked.
>
> "Of course not," he replied. "No fourteen year old is capable of raising a baby. For that matter, not many thirty year olds are qualified. A baby's too difficult for any one person to raise by herself."
>
> "So what do you do with babies?" they asked.
>
> "Well, we baptize them so that we all raise them together. In the case of that fourteen year old, we have given her baby to a retired couple who have enough time and enough wisdom to raise children. They can then raise the mama right along with her baby. That's the way we do it."[2]

This is costly grace. The girl made a big mistake—likely the biggest of her young life—but instead of shunning her or publically humiliating her or reaming her out in the hallway of the church and then walking away in disgust, this church knew how not to let their arrogance turn into condemnation. The people knew that they must help her shoulder the burden. (They must have been reading Paul's writings.) When we shoulder a burden together, then the load will always be lighter. One couple in particular will bear the greater burden of raising the baby and her mama. Yet, if you interviewed them after it was all said and done, I'd bet they'd say that it has been a great honor and a great blessing to them in their retirement.

We've entitled the book *Slow to Judge* in part because of Jesus' message about judgment here. It is not that judgment is always out of bounds or morally wrong. It isn't. Sometimes you must make a judgment in order to help a brother or sister fix the mess he or she has made. Sometimes, and you must be careful here, you must express that judgment to the right people in the right way. But it should never be something you do quickly or without thinking first about your own spiritual condition. Are you spiritually fit to make this call? Are there other spiritually fit folk to help restore that fallen brother? If we are to judge others, we must do it slowly, carefully, after having first examined ourselves, and not until we have truly listened to their story. And judgment is never for any purpose except the possibility of correction and reconciliation. We are not to judge to feel superior to another. We are not to judge in order to damage another's reputation. If we judge at all, we must do so with a deep and sure hope that faults can be mended, relationships restored, and depression

If there is no hope for reconciliation, then there may be no point in expressing our opinion.

lifted. If there is no hope for reconciliation, then there may be no point in expressing our opinion. It may be best to wait a while and pray for a calmer season.

With Paul let us pray that the Father will help us to gently restore the fallen.

QUESTIONS TO CONSIDER:

1. Why is it such a bad idea for Christians to turn to the public courts or public opinions to sort out the churches' problems?

2. If church leaders came to you and asked you to help a brother or sister caught up in some moral failure, would you agree? Why or why not? How would you proceed?

3. Has anyone ever helped you carry a burden of your own making? What kind of burden was it? How do you regard them today?

4. If someone said to you, "Jesus said we shouldn't judge," how would you respond?

A BOOK BY ITS COVER

"Don't judge a book by its cover." When given a chance, most people will surprise you.

I recently had a student take one of my upper-level classes. Her name is Caitlin, and she is a nursing major. One day after class, she and a friend were hanging around, and Caitlin made the statement that she always judges a book by its cover. I laughed and asked her to tell me more. She said it has become somewhat of a sickness for her. She doesn't recall how long she's been doing it, but recently friends showed her how crazy it is. All of her encounters with bookstores had ended the same way. She went in, ran quickly through the fiction section, and then headed for the Christianity/Religion section before pulling a few books from the shelves, sitting on the floor, and then making her final selection. Along the way she would see some ridiculous titles and cover art. Her hard and fast rule was this: any book cover with a grassy field, a beach, or a woman spinning around wearing a flowery skirt could contain nothing but fluff. She cited a few authors and books as examples, but I won't bother you with those.

Well, some of her close friends started reading a few of those authors and books. At first, she gave them a hard time. But over time, those same friends began to wear her down until she picked up one of her cover-banned books and began to read it. She read it once; then she read it again and started recommending it to friends. It was terrific. She's going back to the bookstore and taking a second look at those books. Caitlin thinks she will slowly get over her fear of "crappy cover art," but it's going to be a hard habit to break. Most habits are.

Now the English saying, "Don't judge a book by its cover," is not first of all about books. It's about people. I suppose it could be about books or anything else that presents itself to us at a glance. But those who use the saying typically mean something other than "buy a book only if you like its cover"! It means don't judge people, or anything else for that matter, solely by what they look like on the outside. If you judge them at all, judge them by what is on the inside. And how do you know what is on the inside of someone? Well, eventually what is on the inside makes its way outside in words and actions. So it is words and actions which must be judged, not appearances. Now, this is hard for us to do, if not downright impossible; after all, our society has made judging by appearances into an art form.

Our society has made judging by appearance into an art form.

In May 2014, Naval Adm. William H. McRaven delivered the university-wide commencement address for The University of Texas at Austin. McRaven had graduated from The University of Texas thirty-seven years earlier. Now, after a prestigious career in the military, he came back to impart some wisdom to nearly eight thousand graduates. His commencement address was simple yet brilliant. No doubt students will remember his charge for years to come. Most of his advice came from what he had learned during the rigorous training he endured on his way to becoming a Navy Seal. There was one bit of advice that touches on our topic. Here is an excerpt from his address:

Over a few weeks of difficult training my SEAL class which started with 150 men was down to just 42. There were now six boat crews of seven men each.

I was in the boat with the tall guys, but the best boat crew we had was made up of the little guys—the munchkin crew we called them—no one was over five foot five.

The munchkin boat crew had one American Indian, one African American, one Polish American, one Greek American, one Italian American, and two tough kids from the Midwest.

They out-paddled, out-ran, and out-swam all the other boat crews.

The big men in the other boat crews would always make good-natured fun of the *tiny little flippers* the munchkins put on their *tiny little feet* prior to every swim.

But somehow these little guys, from every corner of the nation and the world, always had the last laugh—swimming faster than everyone and reaching the shore long before the rest of us.

SEAL training was a great equalizer. Nothing mattered but your will to succeed. Not your color, not your ethnic background, not your education, and not your social status.

If you want to change the world, measure a person by the size of their heart, not by the size of their flippers.[1]

How often and how easy it is to take a look at people and think we have them figured out! The color of their skin, the quality of their speech, the cut of their clothing—it is easy to see the size of others' flippers, but much harder to measure the size of their heart. How do you go about that? To do so, you have to spend time with them. You have to watch them. You have to observe what they do and listen to what they say. You have to suspend judgment based simply on appearances. You have to let them be. If you do, then you may well be treated to knowing the real man, the real woman wearing the wee flipper and not just some stereotype.

Martin Luther King Jr. said famously, "I have a dream that my four little children will one day live in a nation where they will not be judged by the color of their skin, but by the content of their character."[2] King's "I Have a Dream" speech was delivered on August 28, 1963 to more than 250,000 people who crowded the steps of the Lincoln Memorial and filled the mall in Washington. Now more than fifty years later, we lament that his dream has not been more fully realized. We've made progress—some think tremendous progress—since those early days of the civil rights movement. But there are still barriers, prejudices, stereotypes, and racial attitudes on all sides which ensure that we will continue to judge a book by its cover. Skin color is often the first thing we see. Tragically, it is often the only thing we see because it demands too much of us to wait and see the content of a person's character. That content will present itself if we will commit ourselves to the hard and arduous task of truly listening to the other and truly watching what becomes of their lives.

I think it is interesting that the admiral made a point to say that the munchkin boat crew was made up of people of various colors, languages, and backgrounds. Why? Because, in the end, those markers were all irrelevant. None of that mattered when it came to accomplishing the mission. Many would have written them off or not taken them seriously simply because they were smaller than the others. But given the chance, they surprised the big fellows and probably their commanders, as well. Together, they surpassed what everyone imagined they could do based upon their size. Size doesn't matter, unless you're talking about size of the heart; but you can only figure that out by being slow to judge and quick to listen.

But society today is hard-wired to prevent that. We demand answers. We demand action. We demand results. We demand them all quickly. "Rush to judgment" has become a well-worn phrase in our degenerating public conversation.

On March 13, 2006, the Duke University lacrosse team hosted a party and hired a few strippers as part of the entertainment (not exactly a wise thing to do). After the party, one of the women (black) accused three of the young men (all white) of sexually assaulting her. Charges were filed and the district attorney took a personal interest in the case. The media quickly fanned the flames of racism (black vs. white) and privilege (poor vs. rich) in their reports. It didn't take much to turn the court of public opinion against the wealthy, white men of Duke based on the woman's accusations. It was as if many wanted to believe her because it fit so well their darkest thoughts about our country. The situation became so dire for Duke's athletic program that the lacrosse coach resigned and the lacrosse season was suspended for the year.

> **We demand answers. We demand action. We demand results. We demand them all quickly.**

But the facts of the case did not support her accusation. Eyewitness reports, strong alibis, contradictory statements, and credibility issues presented clear evidence that the young men were innocent and that the woman had not been raped. She made it all up. Eventually, all the charges were dropped—but not before many people's lives and reputations had been badly damaged. The disgraced district attorney lost his job and was disbarred because of how he bungled the case. Lawsuits were filed against the university, the city of Durham, and the DNA lab for how they conducted themselves during the investigation. Clearly, there had been a rush to judgment by the media and city officials which injured these young men, their families, and their community.[3] They took one look, a brief look, from a wrong perspective, and saw white privilege which must mean that these men were guilty of these horrid crimes. What if those in charge had been slow to judge and quick to listen? What if they had taken enough time to get the facts before they judged the players guilty? Tragically, this kind of rush to judgment takes place all the time in our society. Are there cases where racism raises its ugly head? Absolutely. Are there times where people who've had all the advantages take advantage of the poor? Yes, absolutely. But the Duke lacrosse case was not one of them.

Now, before you think that these events only affected those immediately involved, think again. Not only were those men and their families deeply hurt by the ordeal, but the state of race relations in this country was set back badly by the actions of a few. Until we learn to be slow to judge, until we decide that sometimes it is best to hush up and listen, I'm afraid that a good life and a good society will continue to elude us.

PLAYING FAVORITES

But remember, judgment isn't always negative. Sometimes we look at someone and we like what we see, so we judge them positively based on nothing other than appearance. The admonition "be slow to judge" is not just about judging others negatively; it could also be about judging them positively. Consider James 2:1–9:

> My brothers and sisters, *I know you've heard this before, but* stop playing favorites! Do not try to blend the genuine faith of our glorious Lord Jesus, the Anointed One, *with your silly pretentiousness.* [2] If an affluent gentleman enters your gathering wearing the finest clothes and priceless jewelry, *don't trip over each other trying to welcome him.* And if a penniless bum crawls in with his shabby clothes *and a stench fills the room, don't look away or*

pretend you didn't notice—offer him a seat up front, next to you.
³⁻⁴ If you tell the wealthy man, "Come sit by me; there's plenty of room," but tell the vagrant, "Oh, these seats are saved. Go over there," then you'll be judging *God's children* out of evil motives.

⁵ My dear brothers and sisters, listen: God has picked the poor of this world to become *unfathomably* rich in faith and ultimately to inherit the Kingdom, which He has pledged to those who love Him. ⁶ *By favoring the rich,* you have mocked the poor. *And, correct me if I'm wrong,* but isn't it the rich who step on you while climbing the ladder of success? And isn't it the rich who *take advantage of you and* drag you into court? ⁷ Aren't they the ones mocking the noble name *of our God,* the One calling us?

⁸ *Remember His call, and* live by the royal law found in Scripture: love others as you love yourself. You'll be doing very well if you can get this down. ⁹ But if you show favoritism—*paying attention to those who can help you in some way, while ignoring those who seem to need all the help*—you'll be sinning and condemned by the law.

We are often mesmerized by the rich, powerful, and beautiful people of the world. We dream of associating with them; but when we focus our attention on the fashionable people of this world, it is often at the expense of those who need it the most.

Ignoring the needy and favoring the wealthy is completely contrary to the example Jesus modeled for us while walking on earth. God often chooses those who are the poorest materially to be the richest spiritually. We should welcome everyone equally into God's kingdom, even if it means upsetting boundaries like class and race. The rule is simple: we should treat others in the same way we want to be treated. God does not play favorites, and neither should we.⁴

James is dealing with a real situation, not a hypothetical one. We've all seen it. Some of us are even guilty of it. A person who is clearly wealthy or famous or influential comes into our gathering. He's driving a pricey car, wearing expensive clothing, and carrying himself with the confidence typical of the successful. Quickly, those in charge begin to show him attention which is denied to others, particularly those who come from a more humble station. Showing favoritism to the wealthy or famous is a different way we judge a book by its cover, but it is still being quick to judge. But James wants to make sure that we all get a reality check. They may look good and wear the right cologne. But that's just on the outside. They may have the ability to help us, pull us up a notch or two; but what is on the inside? The inside is bound to come out sooner or later. James reminds us: Isn't it the rich who step on you as they are moving up the ladder of success? Isn't it the influential who drag you into court and make your life miserable if they can gain even a slight advantage? Isn't it the famous who oppress the poor and the marginalized? So why then would God's people ever show favoritism to one over another?

> **In the world that's coming, the rich and mighty are humbled, and the poor and weak are lifted up.**

James's directive here to the church is a no-nonsense one. God is turning the world upside down. Everything is changing, much of it right before our eyes. It started in Bethlehem when a poor virgin gave birth to a son and named Him Jesus. As He grew and matured, He left His father's carpenter shop and took up His heavenly Father's business. He became a herald of the kingdom of God, a radical announcement that the time has come for God to reign as King over all creation. The day has arrived for His will to be done on earth as it is in heaven. We see it demonstrated in various miracles that Jesus performed, when water became wine at a wedding feast in Cana, when the blind saw, when the lame walked, when the demonized were set free, and when the dead stood up and were alive again. The change is not yet complete, but already we sense the King's presence. In the world that's coming, the rich and mighty are humbled, and the poor and weak are lifted up. In God's reign, the poor are made rich in ways that truly matter, and the meek do inherit the earth. That is what God is up to, James insists. So when we or anyone else show favoritism to people simply because they are rich, powerful, or famous, we are mocking the poor whom God favors. When we show hospitality to the wealthy and ignore the poor, we demonstrate how far our values and priorities are from God's.

Instead, James urges us to live by the royal law found in the Scripture. And why is it the royal law? Because this is the law of the King to love others as you love yourself (Lev. 19:18; Matt. 22:39; Mark 12:31; Gal. 5:14). Ultimately, love solves the problem that James addresses, which is our tendency to act favorably toward the rich and pay scant attention to the poor. If we live by the royal law of love, we will lift our heads and "receive the face" (the literal meaning of the Greek word translated above "playing favorites") of both rich and poor.

A few years ago I saw this firsthand when I was serving as a pastor. On a daily basis it was my habit to wear a suit or sport coat and tie. When I dressed down, I put on a nice pair of khakis and a dress shirt. From time to time, I'd have to stop in at our bank. When I did, I would be warmly greeted with a big smile by the bank manager, and the tellers would be attentive to whatever I needed. I loved that bank. Well, one day I realized that I needed to run into the bank, but I hadn't come from work. I had been painting my house in ragged, paint- and dirt-covered shorts and a t-shirt. It was a hot July day, so I was also sweaty and stinky. Same guy, different clothes. When I went into the bank, I expected the same kind of treatment I usually received, but boy was I surprised. Instead of lifting her head and smiling to greet me, the bank manager looked down and walked away quickly. As I made my way to the tellers' stations to make a withdrawal, it was clear that the tellers would rather I go to anyone's window but theirs. When I chose a station and walked up, the teller took a long time getting over to me, though it was clear that he didn't have pressing business. I told him that I wanted to withdraw some money from my account. I gave him a withdrawal slip (it was the dark ages!) and waited as he scrutinized every detail of it. I left the bank that day amazed at the treatment I had received, based solely on how I was dressed. Same guy. Different clothes.

The church ought to be one place where the poor know they can go to be treated like they are friends of the King, because they are.

Don't judge a book by its cover. Right? Who are you kidding? In a small, temporary way I experienced the kind of treatment most people dole out to those who look poor. People look away, ignore them, scrutinize their every move, and give them a hard time when trying to do the slightest thing.

The church ought to be one place where the poor know they can go to be treated like they are friends of the King, because they are. God has made them rich in faith. He has chosen them to shame the so-called wise. He has selected the weak to bring disgrace to those who think they are strong. He has chosen the common and the castoff in order to invalidate those who think they are something (1 Cor. 1:26–31). So when we see them, we should not judge the book by its cover. We should lift our faces, look them in the eye, smile the biggest smile we can, and then listen to what they have to say. We should welcome them to sit alongside us when we gather to worship the one, true God. We should invite them to the best seats at the table when we are enjoying a good cup of coffee or a fine meal.

R-E-S-P-E-C-T

In the Acknowledgments, I mentioned that I have had the privilege of cohosting a radio show in Houston for over a decade. The current version of the show is called *A Show of Faith* (a name suggested by one of my former students). It is on 1070 AM The Answer, a Salem network. I cohost along with a priest and rabbi. No joke! The station is a secular station that has a conservative talk profile, so our show is about events in the news from the standpoint of a Protestant, Catholic, and Jew. That is what we do each week, but another purpose for the show is to demonstrate that people can be friends across faiths—or should I say, despite our faiths. Too often, people get the idea that they can only be friends with people who look like them, think like them, and believe like them. Nothing could be further from the truth. In fact, I count Rabbi Federow and Fathers Mario Arroyo and Brendan Cahill as some of my dearest and most enduring friends. Though we must "agree to disagree," we have found friendship in these conversations and even disagreements.

One night, we had a caller. To be honest, I can't recall what he or she asked, but I remember the answer given by Father Mario. You see, Father Mario is a philosophical theologian. He often pokes fun at Rabbi Stuart and me for going on about the Bible and how we interpret the Bible. He doesn't think the Bible solves many of the questions we have today because of all the different ways it has and can be interpreted. Instead, he thinks the most interesting questions are theological and philosophical. So he keeps bringing us back to those questions. Now, before I leave you with the wrong impression, I must say that he grounds his philosophy and theology in the Bible, but he doesn't engage in endless arguments about what this or that Bible verse means.

Well, Father Mario is a bit of an amateur etymologist (the study of where words come from and what they mean). Mario refers to etymology as the archaeology of words. Often, words mean more than their etymological root, but seldom do they mean less. On this night, Father Mario waxed eloquent about the word *respect*. I'm talking about the word itself, not the Otis Redding song made famous by Aretha Franklin in 1967. In answering the caller's question, the good father referred to the root meaning of the word *respect*. "Re-" means "again," and "spect" comes from a root that means "to look." Father Mario pointed out that the word *spectacles* comes from the same root. So he concluded that the word *respect* means—or ought to mean—that we "look again" or "take a second look."

Often at first glance, we size people up, put them in a category, and then easily dismiss them. This "prejudging" often does not take into account the complexity of what it means to be human. If we truly learn to respect people and their ideas, we will stop and look again. That might mean that we look again and again. Not just a second look, but a third look or maybe more. People, their cultures, and their ideas are seldom one-sided, so it takes us looking from several angles to gain some sense of understanding. Instead, we tend to be quick with our judgments, looking once and often only out of the corner of our eyes. Time is precious, after all, and we need to be able to do things in a snap. So many demands, so little time.

To take a biblical example, imagine if we took a look at King David. Let's sum him up. He is a murderer. He is a mercenary. He is an adulterer. He is a leader who is willing to deceive his people, "I did not have sexual relations with that woman, Ms. Bathsheba." All of these things are true about David, but if we stopped with that, we'd miss something much more important. Despite these failures—and these are deep, serious failures—the Scriptures declare David to be a man after God's heart (1 Sam. 13:14 NKJV; Acts 13:22). Now how can this be? Well, the Scriptures tell us who David is from God's eyes, not our own. After just one slip, some people would count David out. They'd have no more to do with him. But God looked again and again, and what He saw ultimately pleased Him. You see, David repented of the wrong he had done, shed tears over his mistakes, and turned back to a merciful God. So God forgave him. God could see the good in David—a good rooted in His image in all of us—but also demonstrated over and again as David acted faithfully within the covenants God made with him. In a word, God had "respect" for David, made him king, and initiated a covenant with David that ultimately brought the Messiah to redeem and repair the world.

Respect and dignity are due to all people simply because they are made in God's image and likeness.

Now, respect is not easy. Our snap judgments are often confirmed by others. Our Western world is awash with people making quick judgments and then pressing those judgments in our faces on radio, TV, and the Internet. Consider again the Duke lacrosse case. But these pundits in the media often have agendas driving them. It is to their advantage to pigeonhole a person as this or that. We hardly have a chance to breathe.

In the final analysis, true respect and learning to "look again" involves discipline. It involves denying yourself your first impression and then taking the time and effort to stop and listen again. But this is not an age of discipline, at least not when it comes to matters like this. We are expected to form opinions quickly, express opinions boisterously, and never say, "I was wrong." If you do that sort of thing well enough, you may end up with your own radio show. Discipline may be okay when it comes to running marathons or eating healthy, but not when it comes to sizing people up and putting them in a category we can vilify. Conservative, liberal, progressive, fundamentalist, agnostic, atheist, gay, straight, extremist—as one fellow said, labels are for libel.

I've often heard people say, "Respect must be earned, not given." I'm not so sure. A degree can be earned. A job may be earned. A salary may be earned; but respect and dignity are due to all people simply because they are made in God's image and likeness. Respect does not mean that you will always agree with another person. Case in point: I often disagree with Rabbi Federow and my priest friends publically on the radio, but I love and respect them. I take them seriously even when I think they are wrong. As friends, we "agree to disagree but don't become disagreeable." True respect— that is, a willingness to take a second look at another person—is one way we can be slow to judge and quick to listen.

Respect has an interesting quality. It elevates not only the one who gives it, but also the one who receives it. When you respect someone, you elevate them and make them better. Likewise, when you respect someone, you elevate yourself and make yourself better. Show someone respect today and see if others will not surprise you.

With James let us pray that God will help us not play favorites but live instead by the royal law of love.

QUESTIONS TO CONSIDER:

1. Have you ever been misjudged? How did it feel? How did you react?

2. Can you think of times the public has "rushed to judgment"? How about you? What did it take for you to realize you were wrong?

3. What kind of disparity do you see in your church's treatment of the rich and poor, the educated and uneducated, the connected and marginalized? Is there anything you can do to address it?

4. Recall a time in your own life when someone showed you honor and respect. How did that change you?

LOVE AND FORGIVENESS

Every one says forgiveness is a lovely idea, until they have something to forgive.

—C. S. Lewis[1]

On August 31, 1997, Diana, Princess of Wales, was killed in an auto accident in Paris, France as she and her partner Dodi Fayed tried desperately to escape the paparazzi. Her funeral took place six days later in Westminster Abbey in London, a historic site that had witnessed so many royal funerals in the past. More than two thousand people attended the ceremony, while nearly two billion worldwide watched it on TV. It remains one of the most watched events in history.

Those who attended the service, listened on the radio, or watched on television heard Prime Minister Tony Blair read the thirteenth chapter of Paul's first Corinthian letter. The chapter, often referred to as "the love chapter," is frequently read in weddings; it is only occasionally used in funerals. As Blair read from the Authorized Version, he spoke slowly. Every syllable of Paul's weighty words hung in the air and plunged down deep in the soul of a grieving nation.

Love is prerequisite to becoming people who are slow to judge and quick to listen. Unfortunately, the word *love* for us is far too ambiguous. If we hope to understand the Bible's teaching about love, we are going to have to set aside some of our basic assumptions and wrong ideas about it and embrace a more authentic sense of love.

For modern readers, the word *love* is a feeling-oriented word. Love expresses how we feel about things and other people. It is about what or whom we like and what or whom we are attracted to. It is based too much in biology and not enough in serious commitment to God and our neighbor. For modern people, love expresses how we feel about someone and something; authentic Christian love, on the other hand, is an act of the will. It is a choice we make. In America, people use the word *love* in statements as broad as: "I love my wife;" "I love my dog;" "I love my iPad;" "I love my coffee in the morning." Now, what a husband means when he says, "I love my wife," is—or at least it had better be—quite different than when he says, "I love my dog" or "I love my car."

It is easy to love everyone in general and no one in particular.

In 1995, Budweiser introduced a series of commercials based on the tagline "I Love You, Man." The first commercial featured a scruffy-looking fellow named Johnny sitting on a pier, fishing with his father. Johnny moves over toward his dad and says with deep emotion in his voice, "Dad. Well, you're my dad. And I love you, man." The father shrinks back suspiciously and says, "You're not getting my Bud Light, Johnny." As the announcer is extolling the great taste and other virtues of the brew, Johnny cuts his eyes to his right and moves over to another man, seated on the pier. Johnny says, "Ray?" but before he can finish his heartfelt speech, Ray responds, "Forget it, Johnny." The campaign was clearly successful, for in 1996 Charlton Heston agreed to appear with Johnny in one of the commercials. As a result of the campaign, the phrase "I love you, man" made its way into common speech. People were saying it in all sorts of contexts, and the phrase "I love you" or phrases like "love ya" became common not only among family but also friends and acquaintances.

I don't know about you, but I've had people say "love ya" when it felt forced or a bit awkward because I hardly knew them. I've often heard Hollywood actors stand before a televised audience at an awards ceremony to express thanks; they typically end their speech: "I love you all." You do? Really? You don't even know me, and yet you love me? You see, it is easy to love everyone in general and no one in particular. But love must be particular. Love must have an object. And the object of love is often a particular person who is imperfect, flawed, and occasionally a real mess. My point is that a word like *love* can have so many meanings that it is almost meaningless. So when we turn to the Bible and read about love, we have to distinguish carefully what the Scriptures are trying to tell us.

There are different words translated "love" in the Bible. Each word has a different range of meanings (what linguists call "semantic fields"). The word I want to discuss here is the Greek word *agapé* because it is the word translated "love" in the famous love chapter read by Prime Minister Blair during Princess Diana's funeral. What we know about this word—both as a noun and a verb—is that it is action-oriented, not feeling-oriented. It is not about how we feel about someone or something, but how we act toward them. That act begins in the will, as the Catholic Catechism says: "To love is to will the good of another" (statement 1766). But to will something is not to wish it; it is to desire it so deeply that a course of action is set. And what is that action? Seeking the good of another—*good*, that is, as defined by God, not as defined by society.

Take, for example, John 3:16 ("For God so loved the world . . . ." NKJV). The word *love* here has nothing to do with how God *felt* about the world, but how God *acted* toward the world. In The Voice, we tried to capture the heart of it in our translation, "For God expressed His love for the world in this way: He gave His only Son so that whoever believes in Him will not face everlasting destruction, but will have everlasting life." This is how God loved the world: He gave His only Son. Frankly, we don't know how God felt about the world. Did God have a warm, fuzzy feeling about the world? Was He aggravated and put off by what He saw? Did God feel sorry for what people were going through? We just don't know. By and large, how God felt is irrelevant. What is relevant is what God did for us through His Son. Put another way, people don't receive the gift of everlasting life because God had a loving feeling; they are saved because God expressed a loving act in sending His only Son.

Now to be honest, it is much easier to love the people you like. That is a given. But Scripture does not say, "Love the people you like as you love yourselves." No, it says, "Love your neighbor as you love yourselves." Your neighbor may be someone whom you like, or he may be someone whom you don't really know, or he could be someone who has acted deliberately to hurt you. This is why Christians are called to engage in great personal risk: love your enemies and speak blessings on those who persecute you (Matt. 5:43–48; Luke 6:27–28). Now, this will entail forgiveness, and we must talk about this later. For now, it is enough to say that loving your neighbor is an act of the will to do them good (and not harm). Love will pursue what is best for them, regardless of the cost.

C. S. Lewis makes an important point when he urges Christ followers not to waste time wondering whether you love your neighbor. He advises: simply act as if you do. If you do this, you will unlock one of the great secrets of your spiritual lives. When you act as if you love someone, you will soon discover that you actually do love them. Regrettably, the same spiritual law also works in reverse. Writing not long after the end of World War II, Lewis notes, "The Germans, perhaps, at first ill-treated the Jews because they hated them: afterwards they hated them much more because they had ill-treated them. The more cruel you are, the more you will hate; and the more you hate, the more cruel you will become—and so on in a vicious circle forever."[2] Sadly, the world is filled with hatred and cruelty. Tune in to any hour in the 24-hour news cycle and see how pervasive it is. By acting vengefully, people guarantee that the fight will be on again tomorrow and the next day and the next. Something radical must happen in order to break the cycle, and the Christian faith has the right prescription if we are courageous enough to live by it: love your neighbor as you love yourself, love your enemies, and speak a blessing over those who have treated you horribly. And loving your neighbors will mean that you treat them kindly and do to them what you would want done to you. This is why we've insisted that loving your neighbor is prerequisite to being slow to judge and quick to listen.

As you read the famous love passage, set aside any thought that creeps in that love is about what we are attracted to or what we like or how we feel toward someone or something. None of that is relevant; it is how we act toward others, what we do for others, that matters.

> What if I speak in the *most elegant* languages of people or in the *exotic* languages of the heavenly messengers, but I live without love? Well then, anything I say is like the clanging of brass or a crashing cymbal. [2] What if I have the gift of prophecy, am blessed with knowledge and insight to all the mysteries, or what if my faith is strong enough to scoop a mountain *from its bedrock*, yet I live without love? If so, I am nothing. [3] I could give all that I have to feed the poor, I could surrender my body to be burned *as a martyr*, but if I do not live in love, I gain nothing *by my selfless acts.*
>
> [4] Love is patient; love is kind. Love isn't envious, doesn't boast, *brag, or strut about.* There's no arrogance in love; [5] it's

never rude, crude, or indecent—it's not self-absorbed. Love isn't easily upset. Love doesn't tally wrongs [6] or celebrate injustice; but truth—*yes, truth*—is love's delight! [7] Love puts up with anything and everything that comes along; it trusts, hopes, and endures no matter what. [8] Love will never become obsolete. Now as for the prophetic gifts, they will not last; unknown languages will become silent, and the gift of knowledge will no longer be needed. [9] Gifts of knowledge and prophecy are partial at best, *at least for now,* [10] but when the perfection *and fullness of God's kingdom* arrive, all the parts will end. [11] When I was a child, I spoke, thought, and reasoned in childlike ways *as we all do.* But when I became a man, I left my childish ways behind. [12] For now, we can only see a dim and blurry picture of things, as when we stare into polished metal. I realize that everything I know is only part of the big picture. But one day, *when Jesus arrives,* we will see clearly, face-to-face. In that day, I will fully know just as I have been wholly known *by God.* [13] But now faith, hope, and love remain; these three *virtues must characterize our lives.* The greatest of these is love. (I Cor. 13:1–13)

Paul boils it all down for the believers in Corinth. Religious people often spend their time practicing rituals, projecting dogma, and going through routines that might look like Christianity on the outside but that lack the essential ingredient that brings all of it together—love! It is a loving God who birthed creation and now pursues a broken people in the most spectacular way. That same love must guide believers, so faith doesn't appear to be meaningless noise.[3]

Paul's exposé on love sits at the heart of his discussion about spiritual gifts (1 Cor. 12–14). Apparently, some in Corinth had written Paul a letter asking about these special *charisms* (from the Greek word often translated *gift*). First Corinthians 12–14 is the apostle's answer. Now, we don't have the Corinthians' letter to Paul, so we don't know the question they asked, but we do have Paul's answer.

In chapter 12, the apostle instructs the Corinthians that there are many kinds of spiritual gifts, but the variety of gifts come from the same God and serve a single, significant purpose—namely, each gift is given for the good of the whole community. They are not for anyone's private enjoyment or benefit. God has gifted each baptized believer with a special *charism* that manifests the Spirit's power and joins them into the body of Christ. Every person has a gift and a role to play as a member of that body. On the surface, some gifts may seem more important, but when you look deeper, you realize that every gift is essential to the well-being of the body. This means that the gifts and gifted are mutually dependent on one another. Each gift can and ought to be celebrated. Paul ends the chapter with this directive (12:31), "Pursue the greater gifts, and let me tell you of a more excellent way—*love*."

For Paul, love is not one of the spiritual gifts, it is the "more excellent way." Gifts will vary from person to person, but everyone must exercise his or her gift in love. Love is the road down which the gifts must travel on their way to building up the church. Love is the atmosphere in which all the gifts are to be exercised. That is why Paul begins this chapter as he does. If I speak in various languages but don't have love, then it is all noise and chatter. If I use my prophetic gifts without love, then I am nothing and I accomplish nothing. If I

> **If I speak in various languages but don't have love, then it is all noise and chatter.**

play the part of a martyr but don't have love, then nothing and no one is gained by my actions. Again, love is the way the gifts must be put into service in order to build up Christ's body.

When Paul talks about the character of love, we need to pay attention, for character always manifests itself in conduct. He lays these out briefly yet profoundly:

> [4] Love is patient; love is kind. Love isn't envious, doesn't boast, *brag, or strut about.* There's no arrogance in love; [5] it's never rude, crude, or indecent—it's not self-absorbed. Love isn't easily upset. Love doesn't tally wrongs [6] or celebrate injustice; but truth—*yes, truth*—is love's delight! [7] Love puts up with anything and everything that comes along; it trusts, hopes, and endures no matter what. [8] Love will never become obsolete. (1 Cor. 13:4–8)

Consider our theme—slow to judge and quick to listen—over and against love's character and conduct. **Love is patient**; literally, it suffers long. It resists those natural feelings of anger, frustration, and indignation, which most people experience and act on. **Love is kind.** It extends good to others and exhibits a gracious, caring disposition. **Love is not envious** or jealous when someone has a clear advantage. **Love doesn't boast, brag, or strut about.** It doesn't show off or call attention to itself. **Love is never rude, crude, or indecent. It is not self-absorbed.** It focuses on the good *in* others and good *for* others. **Love is not easily upset.** It makes allowances for the faults of others. It isn't prone to irritation and biting sarcasm. **Loves does not tally wrongs.** There are no records kept, no ledgers filled, no airing of grievances. Love forgives and releases the offender. **Love puts up with anything and everything that comes along.** It doesn't vent against others and the world. It bears up in silence and never points out all it has had to endure. Love covers a multitude of sins (1 Peter 4:8 NKJV). **Love trusts** in the good of others without being gullible. It looks for and finds the good in all people, simply because all people are made in the image and likeness of God. **Love hopes** and keeps hoping when most people have given up. It can do so because it places its trust ultimately in God and His Son who said, "Don't get lost in despair; believe in God, and keep on believing in Me" (John 14:1). **Love endures no matter what. Love will never become obsolete.** It is never out of place, out of touch, or out of sync; it is never unwelcome. No matter what, love will survive.

Paul ends the love passage in a memorable way. Spiritual gifts, he says, are destined to cease when Christ returns. As long as we live in this broken age, however, we need them even if the benefits they offer only help us to see "a dim and blurry picture of things, as when we stare into polished metal. . . . But one day, *when Jesus arrives*, we will see clearly, face-to-face. In that day, I will fully know just as I have been wholly known *by God*" (1 Cor. 13:12). So at the second coming of Jesus, all the spiritual gifts which have instructed and nurtured the church will come to an end. They will no longer be needed, for the immediate presence of Jesus will render every other grace-gift null and void. But—and this is a big *but*—three things will remain. Three virtues will accompany us into everlasting life: faith, hope, and love. These Christian virtues will never become obsolete. There will never be a time when we can be without them. In the world to come, we will need faith, hope, and love. And the greatest of these is love.

FORGIVENESS

Not long ago, I was talking with Craig Keener about his book *Miracles: The Credibility of the New Testament Accounts*.[4] He was giving a series of presentations on the topic to PhD students at B. H. Carroll Theological Institute in Arlington, TX. Scholars typically classify the miracles performed by Jesus in the Gospels as four types: (a) exorcisms, (b) healings, (c) nature miracles, and (d) resuscitations. In my response to Keener, I said that I think we should add another, a fifth class of miracle, to the list: the miracle of forgiveness.

Before you object too loudly and say, "forgiveness is not a miracle," hear me out. Restoring sight to a blind man or walking on the water or resuscitating Lazarus are miracles. They are unusual happenings, remarkable signs reflecting the presence and priorities of God's kingdom. And regardless of what you think a miracle is—a violation of natural law or the invocation of some higher law—when you think how unlikely forgiveness is, how truly rare it is, and how incredibly hard it is, you may agree with me that for someone to actually forgive another takes a supra-normal act of God. Normal is to hold grudges. Normal is to want to get back at the one who hurt you. Normal is to nurse your wounds and seek revenge, but to forgive another is beyond normal. It is extraordinary, and miracles are extraordinary events. Forgiveness requires God's action in us to overcome our normal, natural tendencies to want to settle the score.

For someone to actually forgive another takes a supra-normal act of God.

Now, I'm bracketing off God's forgiveness of our sins for now. It is a given that for God to forgive us for all we have done against Him, His creation, and each other takes an act of God. That's not my concern. I'm concerned here about the need we all have to forgive and to be forgiven. In the Lord's Prayer, Jesus urged His disciples to pray, "And forgive us our debts as we forgive those who owe us something" (Matt. 6:12). He goes on to explain the connection between God's forgiveness of us and our forgiveness of others, "If you forgive people when they sin against you, then your Father will forgive you *when you sin against Him and when you sin against your neighbor.* But if you do not forgive your neighbors' sins, your Father will not forgive your sins" (vv. 14–15).

Take a moment and consider how rare true forgiveness is and how difficult it is to achieve. Many Christians I know can look back over their lives to see a great deal of relational wreckage brought on mostly because few know how or are willing to forgive. There are plenty of reasons for this: forgiveness is hard to do; everyone is waiting for the other person to admit his or her mistake first; and (then there's the big one) we're not really convinced that forgiveness and reconciliation are necessary for us to live a Christ-centered life. We think we can get along pretty well with relational wreckage littering our past. After all, it was mostly the other guy's fault. Oh, don't get me wrong. We know that God's forgiveness of us is necessary—we pretty much insist on it—but we're not willing to extend the same courtesy to others.

C. S. Lewis quipped, "Every one says forgiveness is a lovely idea, until they have something to forgive, as we had during the war."[5] I suppose forgiving the little things might seem mundane enough, but what about the big things: the World Wars, the Holocaust, the genocide in Rwanda, 9/11, the school shooting in Connecticut, an act of betrayal in marriage, sexual abuse of a child? To suggest that those hurt most by a war crime or an atrocity or a betrayal need to forgive their killers or betrayers is to invite ridicule and hateful stares. How dare you suggest such a thing! Well, it's not me; it's the gospel. And some people take the gospel seriously.

On May 13, 1981, Pope John Paul II was making his way through St. Peter's Square in an open motorcade when a Turkish terrorist, Mehmet Ali Agca, slipped up to the car and shot the pope six times at close range. The pope lost a great deal of blood and would have died had it not been for prompt medical care. After he recovered, John Paul II went to visit his would-be assassin in prison in Rome during the Christmas season of 1983. When the pope arrived at his cell, he looked him in the eye and shook the hand that pulled the trigger. Agca responded by kissing the hand of the pope. They talked quietly together for more than twenty minutes. To this day, no one but Agca knows what passed between them. After the pope told him that he forgave him, he handed Agca a small gift, a rosary made of silver and mother-of-pearl. Lewis Smedes writes: "Forgiveness happens inside the person doing the forgiving. It heals our pain and resentment before it does anything for the person we forgive; they might never know about it."[6] The pope knew well the demands of the gospel. He not only preached forgiveness, he lived it large before God and the world.

The assassination attempt was captured on film and in classic photographs from the time. They can be seen on the Internet. When Pope John Paul II went to visit Agca in prison, he took along a photographer and a film crew to record this historic moment. The pope knew that the images of the assassination attempt had been etched into the hearts and minds of people around the world. Now he wanted a new set of images to emerge from the prison to inspire the world and give us all a lesson in forgiveness. A world obsessed with violence and unforgiving hatreds desperately needed to watch what the pope was about to do. This startling drama of reconciliation and forgiveness rests, I believe, on a miracle of forgiveness that started in the heart of a pope and ultimately addressed the world. In February 2005, when the aged pope was in the hospital fighting the flu, Agca reached out to him and sent him a note wishing him a speedy recovery. A few weeks later, Pope John Paul II died.

Closer to home, the world witnessed another amazing act of forgiveness. On October 2, 2006, Charles Carl Roberts IV entered a one-room schoolhouse in the Old Order Amish community of

Nickel Mines, a village in Lancaster County, Pennsylvania. Roberts, whom the Amish knew as the milk truck driver, took hostages and shot ten young girls at close range (aged 6–13) before turning the gun on himself. When the crisis was over, five girls were dead as well as the shooter. In the aftermath of the shootings, the world was stunned to learn that the Amish were already beginning to forgive the murderer. Dramatically, one day after parents buried their children killed in the attack, several grief-stricken Amish families attended the burial service of the shooter to try to comfort the widow and other members of her family. A year later, the Amish community donated money to help the widow and her children with the financial burdens left when their father killed himself. Before you get the idea that the Amish just got over it quickly, you need to realize that they suffered nightmares and post-traumatic stress, and many even began going to counseling (an odd admission for those who don't use electricity or drive cars). The horrible events that took place at the old school house meant that they could no longer use the building, so the community came together to tear it down and build another. No, the Amish loved their children as much as anyone else; they didn't just get over it and move on. They dealt with the tragedy the way anyone else would have, except for this one thing: they believed the gospel of forgiveness. Those who know the Amish best realize that, because they can forgive, because they refuse to hold grudges, they are well suited to begin the process of healing and putting their lives back together.[7]

> **Forgiveness . . . heals our pain and resentment before it does anything for the person we forgive.**
>
> **—Lewis Smedes**

So let's consider what forgiveness is and what it does. Then we will see how important forgiveness is to loving our enemies and becoming the kind of people that are slow to judge and quick to listen. We have to think about this in two ways: what does it mean for the offended? What does it mean for the offender? Let's begin with what forgiveness does to you if you have been hurt or injured by someone. In the New Testament, the word *forgiveness* comes from a root which means "to let go." In a real sense, forgiveness involves letting go of the offense and releasing the offender from the debt he owes you. In the early years of our radio show, Rabbi Federow and I interviewed Rabbi Harold Kushner about his book *How Good Do We Have to Be?*[8] At the time, Kushner was probably the most significant Jewish voice in America. His earlier book *When Bad Things Happen to Good People*[9] had thrust him on the national stage as one of the most articulate spokesmen for Jews and Judaism. The conversation that evening turned to the topic of forgiveness, and I will never forget what the rabbi said. Kushner said that forgiveness is a favor that we first do for ourselves and second for the other person. The opposite of forgiveness is to hold a grudge and to try to keep someone indebted to you. This is a miserable place to be for many reasons. According to Kushner, holding a grudge is like standing around with a hot coal in your hand waiting for the offender to walk by so you can fling it at him. In the meantime, all you get is a burned hand.

> **Forgiveness is not an admission that the offended was the one at fault.**

Depending on the character of the offender, he may be oblivious to your hurt or he may not care. In either case, while you're waiting to get back at him, he is no worse for wear.

Before we say more about what forgiveness is, let's be clear what forgiveness is not. First, forgiveness is not an admission that the offended was the one at fault. Some offenders may wish to turn it around and twist it that way: "Well, I only said what I did because you did what you did. You're the one to blame." No, taking the blame when you were not at fault is not forgiveness.

Second, forgiveness does not mean that what the offender did was not all that bad. It may be easier to forgive a light offense, but just because you forgive someone does not mean that what the offender did was not wrong and did not hurt you deeply. Pretending the offense wasn't that big a deal is not forgiveness.

Third, forgiveness does not mean that you sweep the offense under the rug hoping it will go away one day. Ignoring a wrong committed won't make it go away. You cannot ignore it forever. Oh, you may be able to ignore it for a time, but deep down it will continue to fester in your soul. Eventually, it will rear its ugly head when you least expect. Ignoring a wrong committed against you and not dealing with it is not forgiveness.

Fourth, forgiveness does not mean that no price has to be paid. Forgiveness does not negate the consequences of actions taken, words spoken. A man may forgive another man who attacked him violently, but still sleep a bit sounder knowing that his attacker is in jail. Likewise, a woman may truly forgive a husband who abused her, but then make the decision that it is best for them to live separately for a while. Forgiveness recognizes the gravity of sins and their consequences. It is in society's best interest to deal with crime through a system of justice. It is in your best interest to forgive the person who is caught up in that system.

So what is forgiveness? It is letting go of an offense committed against you for the express purposes of (a) freeing yourself from the bondage and injury brought on by holding grudges, and (b) releasing the offender from the debt he or she owes you. It is getting to a place where you can think about that person without thinking about how he hurt you. Ultimately, it is arriving at a moment in time when you treat him and deal with him as if the injury never even occurred.

I submit that, for this to take place, it takes a supernormal act of God in a person's life; it takes a miracle.

Yet forgiveness is seldom instantaneous. It rarely happens automatically. Most people struggle to forgive even light offenses. Forgiveness then is a process we agree to enter under the grace and mercy of God, trusting that one day we will be free from the hurt. It begins with an act of the will to forgive another. It continues as we choose daily to let go of the offense. And then, gloriously, miraculously, one day we will wake up and realize that we have indeed let it go; we have forgiven our debtor. The offense which once occupied so much of our mental energy is now gone because we have been able to let it go. The offender who at one time took up so much of our thought is no longer an enemy because we have released him from his debt. No longer do we hope that something bad will happen to him. Now we wish him nothing but good, God's goodness.

> **Gloriously, miraculously, one day we will wake up and realize that we have indeed let it go; we have forgiven our debtor.**

None of this is possible without God's miraculous intervention. As we continually experience God's love and forgiveness in our own lives, as we regularly pray the Lord's prayer with those haunting words "and forgive us our debts as we forgive those who owe us something," we are sure to be transformed into forgiving people (Matt. 6:12). That transformation may take months or years, but it will always come.

When hurt and injury come between you and another, there is no willingness to listen to anything except an apology. Until you deal redemptively with the pain and the offense, no kind word can pass between you. Regardless of what good the other does, you will continue to judge them harshly until the miracle of forgiveness takes root in you and brings genuine relief and peace. This is why forgiveness is essential to reconciliation. We cannot be at peace with others, we will not be slow to judge and quick to listen, as long as we refuse to reconcile with one another.

CAST THE FIRST STONE

One of the most memorable and celebrated examples of Jesus' forgiveness is found in John's Gospel (8:1–11).

Jesus went to the Mount of Olives. [2] He awoke early in the morning to return to the temple. *When He arrived,* the people surrounded Him, so He sat down and began to teach them. [3] *While He was teaching,* the scribes and Pharisees brought in a woman who was caught in the act of adultery; and they stood her before Jesus.

PHARISEES: [4] Teacher, this woman was caught in the act of adultery. [5] Moses says in the law that we are to kill such women by stoning. What do You say about it?

[6] This was all set up as a test for Jesus; His answers would give them grounds to accuse Him *of crimes against Moses' law.* Jesus bent over and wrote something in the dirt with His finger. [7] They persisted in badgering Jesus, so He stood up straight.

JESUS: Let the first stone be thrown by the one among you who has not sinned.

[8] Once again Jesus bent down to the ground and resumed writing with His finger. [9] The Pharisees who heard Him *stood still for a few moments and then* began to leave slowly, one by one, beginning with the older men. Eventually only Jesus and the woman remained, [10] and Jesus looked up.

JESUS: *Dear* woman, where is everyone? *Are we alone?* Did no one step forward to condemn you?

WOMAN CAUGHT IN ADULTERY: " Lord, no one *has condemned me.*

JESUS: Well, I do not condemn you either; *all I ask is that you go* and from now on avoid the sins that plague you.

Right in the middle of Jesus' lesson in the temple, some of Jesus' detractors challenged His honor and tried to get the best of Him. They burst on the scene dragging a woman they had caught in the act of adultery. They wanted Jesus to pass judgment on her quickly and publicly based on the Mosaic law. They knew well that the law said if any were caught in adultery, they deserved to die. They knew, too, that Jesus had made sinners His friends and that He hung out with unsavory types like tax collectors and fishermen. They figured that if Jesus immediately sided with the law and called for her stoning, it would put Him crossways with many in His audience.

But notice, where is the man she was supposedly with? He is nowhere in sight. Perhaps he got off scot-free or perhaps he escaped and slipped into the back of the crowd to see what would happen. Has the woman been set up just so they could trip up Jesus? Or is this just typical male privilege in a world of double standards? We don't know. What we do know is that Jesus' opponents are exercising selective justice. If she was caught in the act, then there must have been a man there. According to Moses' law, when a man commits adultery with his neighbor's wife, both offenders must be punished (Lev. 20:10). Like a lot of men at that time (and even now), Jesus' opponents were operating with a double standard. The man gets off scot-free while the woman pays heavily for her sins. It was and is a despicable corruption of God's good law. But Jesus knew the score and would have none of it.

So He stooped down and began writing in the dirt. No one knows what Jesus was writing. Was He simply doodling in the dust? Or was He writing something specific? Was He naming names of the women they had slept with? Was He simply killing time? The point is: He didn't answer quickly. He didn't take the bait in this game of honor and shame. Then He stood and said in effect, "Let's get this started. The first stone is to be thrown by the one who has not sinned." Then He stooped down again and continued writing in the dust. One by one, the woman's accusers filed away, starting with the oldest. They were disappointed. They figured out pretty quickly that they wouldn't be getting the best of Jesus this day. Jesus was the only one qualified to cast the first stone, and He refused to do so. Eventually, it was just Jesus and the woman left standing there. No one was prepared to condemn her. Jesus said that He would not condemn her to death either, but He didn't condone her sin. Adultery is serious business, so He urged her to never again commit this sin.

Jesus was the only one qualified to cast the first stone, and He refused to do so.

This is an amazing story. It is one of my favorites because it illustrates perfectly how slow God is to anger and how eager He is to forgive. We imagine that God is up in heaven watching our every move just waiting for us to foul up so He has an excuse to "smite" us. What we discover in this story is that God the Son refuses to condone sin, but He is not ready to cast the first stone. I wonder what kind of impression Jesus left that day on the crowd who witnessed this. I wonder, too, what lesson Jesus had been teaching when He was so rudely interrupted. Imagine sitting at the feet of Jesus and listening to Him teach, when this mob crashes in and throws this woman down between you and

Jesus. Whatever the lesson was, I'm sure it was quickly forgotten in all the drama that followed.

Often, we teach with our actions. That is what Jesus did that day. He said little. He did nothing but write quietly in the dust. He forgave much without giving in and diminishing the gravity of her transgression. She had crossed a line, a serious line, but perhaps she knew that even as she was in the act. So Jesus sent her away: "Go home to your husband. Go home to your children. *And* don't let this sin plague you any longer."

ONE PERSON WE LOVE

Now, it is perfectly normal and right for us to "hate the sin but love the sinner." It is sub-Christian to call injustice justice or to ignore treachery or to pay no attention to human trafficking. We must hate it because God does. And we hate it precisely because we love our neighbor. If we want what is best for him, then we would wish on him none of these things. Now, hating the sin and loving the sinner may be hard, but it is not impossible. As Jud Wilhite, pastor of Central Christian Church in Las Vegas, writes:

> . . . there is someone I love, even though I don't approve of
> what he does. There is someone I accept, though some of his
> thoughts and actions revolt me. There is someone I forgive,
> though he hurts the people I love the most. That person is *me*.
> There are plenty of things I do that I don't like, but if I can love
> myself without approving of all I do, I can also love others with-
> out approving all they do.[10]

Since there is at least one person that we love even as we hate the sin—that is, ourselves—we can certainly learn to do the same for our neighbors, since we are called to love our neighbors as ourselves.

If we are to become the kind of people who are slow to judge and quick to listen, then we must recognize how important love and forgiveness will be in our own personal journeys. If we refuse to love, then we will be quick to judge and have no interest in what our neighbors or our enemies have to say. To judge someone quickly is to exchange love for apathy or worse. To refuse to listen to another is no different than deciding to hold something against them. Love and forgiveness are going to demand a different, riskier approach. Love will make us vulnerable to others even as forgiveness will release our debtor. But the love we have described is not based in feelings; it is based in an act of the will to treat others kindly, to do them good, and to pursue what is in their best interests regardless of the cost. This is the same kind of love which God demonstrated to us by sending His Son in the likeness of human flesh in order to liberate us from all that binds us.

With the church let us pray that God will help us love others as we love ourselves and grant us the grace to love and forgive our enemies.

QUESTIONS TO CONSIDER:

1. Why is it important to focus on love as an action rather than a feeling? How does this run counter to the way most people think of love?

2. How do you recommend people find their spiritual gifts? Have you ever witnessed someone exercising their gifts without love?

3. Have you ever experienced real forgiveness? Do you agree that real forgiveness takes a miracle? Why or why not?

4. Why is forgiving ourselves sometimes more difficult than forgiving others?

5. Who are you having trouble forgiving? What would it take for the miracle of forgiveness to take root in you?

HOMOPHOBIA, ISLAMOPHOBIA, CHRISTOPHOBIA

Don't let even one rotten word seep out of your mouths. Instead, offer only fresh words that build others up when they need it most. That way your good words will communicate grace to those who hear them.

—Paul (Eph. 4:29)

fter reading the chapter title, I bet you are thinking, "What is a chapter like this doing here?" Well, it is fairly simple. I'm convinced that, if we are going to be slow to judge and quick to listen, we must understand that the words we hear and the words we use matter. A word can either foster conversation or stop it cold. That is especially true of some of the labels currently in use.

Take all of the current "–phobia" words out there. If a person expresses a belief that homosexual acts are inherently wrong or disordered, that person is branded *homophobic*. If a person points out that a great deal of the terrorism perpetrated against Muslims, Christians, and Jews in the last thirty years has come from Muslim extremists, that person is pronounced guilty of *Islamophobia*. Christians have even gotten in on the act. When someone criticizes some long-held belief or moral stance of orthodox Christianity, those critics are called *Christophobic.*

A few years ago, such words did not exist, even though the realities they represent have existed for a long time. Since Christianity emerged in the first century, followers of Jesus have expressed moral disapproval of homosexual acts. This has been the mainstream view in the West until recently, as codified in most American states in their sodomy laws. After Muslims conquered Damascus and occupied the Holy Land, Christians criticized the spread of Islam "by the sword." Since the Enlightenment, agnostics and atheists alike have disparaged Christian faith and practice as retrograde. A new brand of atheism has become increasingly aggressive and some would say "evangelistic" during the last decade of the twentieth century.

If the reality and the sentiments are not new, what is? The rhetoric is new and the political power has shifted. With words such as *homophobia, Islamophobia,* and *Christophobia,* we can cast a broad net of disapproval over groups of people. Without taking seriously what another person is saying and why they are saying it—without respecting them as persons—then we quickly shove them into some hated category.

When you stop and think about these new words, they are in fact strange words to be sure. The root "–phobia" comes from Greek. It means "fear of" something. It is a useful term when used correctly. There are a number of disorders which psychologists describe as panic or fear disorders. People who are agoraphobic,

> Without taking seriously what another person is saying and why they are saying it—without respecting them as persons—then we quickly shove them into some hated category.

for example, have a fear of leaving safe places (like their homes) and venturing off into wider, open places like markets and other public spaces. Claustrophobics have a real fear of being cooped up in small places, either alone or with other people. Glossophobia involves a panic response to public speaking. I have occasionally had students come to my office and weep uncontrollably prior to having to present their research before classmates. Triskaidekaphobics have a fear of the number 13. Perhaps you've been in buildings where there was no thirteenth floor. Apparently, the architects had a touch of triskaidekaphobia or at least they were a bit superstitious about such matters. But true phobias come with severe physical responses: adrenaline and other chemicals are pumped into your bloodstream, your heart races, your muscles tense, your breathing quickens, your blood vessels constrict, and your mind gets a bit muddled because all you can think about is getting away from whatever threat is causing the panic.

I'm hard-pressed to see how the current, in-vogue uses of homophobia, Islamophobia, or Christophobia have anything to do with fear, nor do they add anything useful to the public conversation about important matters facing us. Frankly, it diminishes people who struggle with true psychological disorders and co-opts a term useful in the psychological sciences for political or power purposes. If we need a new word—and I don't doubt we do—I'd much rather see us create words which mean something and speak the truth about what people believe and do. I'm convinced that we are all after a good life and a good society. We just disagree about what a good life or a good society looks like. That's why we need to talk with and not at each other. Unfortunately, the talk radio phenomenon of confrontation rather than conversation has taken over most dialogue, even private ones. However, in an age of Facebook and Twitter, what one person says to another in an unguarded moment could well end up spreading to hundreds if not thousands. So what do we do? Out of fear, we sit down and shut up and we avoid controversy.

On the other hand, what are we to make of the extreme responses we see to homosexuality, Islam, and Christianity in small sectors of society? The Westboro Baptist Church, for example, is an unaffiliated church in Topeka, Kansas; it is often in the news for conducting anti-gay protests at military funerals and for picketing high profile, public events. The small church of approximately forty members is composed primarily of the extended family of Fred Phelps who served as its leader until his death in March, 2014.[1] The largest Baptist bodies in the world—members of the Baptist World Alliance and the Southern Baptist Convention—have denounced the church in no uncertain terms.[2] Classified as a hate group by many newspapers and the Southern Poverty Law Center,[3] the church's activities are monitored closely by the Anti-Defamation League.[4] Now, is fear of homosexuality what is driving the Westboro Baptist Church? They don't seem to be afraid of much. Indeed, if you listen carefully to their own words, it is hatred of homosexuals and their sexual activities that arouses them. Browse their statements and literature and you will see how often the word *hate* occurs. So is homophobia the best way to categorize their attitude toward homosexuality? Not really.

A second problem has to do with how limiting a word like *homophobia* is. There is no way to distinguish levels or degrees of "homophobia." A Catholic bishop who has reasoned, principled arguments against same-sex marriage based on tradition and history can be branded homophobic, but so can members of the Westboro Baptist Church. But I think most reasonable people would see a world of difference between them. Perhaps there is no flexibility or nuance to such a word because those who use it don't want there to be. They want to paint with the broadest brush possible. So the position of a Catholic bishop who opposes same-sex marriage is categorized with the people picketing at a funeral of a fallen soldier with signs that demean homosexuals and claim America is doomed because of them. To be anywhere close to accurate, we'd need to develop some scale, say one to ten. According to this system, a Catholic bishop would be described as a first-degree homophobe, while people carrying signs in public places declaring God hates homosexuals would be tenth-degree homophobes. I'm kidding, of course, but it underscores the nature of the problem. All opposition to homosexuality, Islam, and Christianity is not alike. As long as we insist on using inaccurate words in a capricious way, we are never going to make any real progress toward a less judgmental, more peaceful society.

And what of extreme responses to Islam? Terry Jones became infamous in 2010 for his plan to burn Qurans. He is the pastor of the Dove World Outreach Center, an independent church located in Florida.[5] Believing that Islam is a violent religion that threatens to impose its own brand of justice in America, Jones wrote a controversial book entitled *Islam Is of the Devil.* But it was not until he announced plans to burn Qurans on social media in July 2010 that Jones received international attention. The announcement itself was enough to set off a firestorm of protests all over the world. General David Petraeus, commander of the International Security Assistance Force in Afghanistan, and President Obama warned that extreme elements in Islam would use the threat as an excuse to attack Americans all over the world.[6] Jones canceled the

> As long as we insist on using inaccurate words in a capricious way, we are never going to make any real progress toward a less judgmental, more peaceful society.

event, initially believing that he could broker a deal to have the Park 51 mosque moved from Ground Zero. But when that did not materialize, he held a mock trial of the Quran in March 2011 and burned a copy of it for "crimes against humanity." Reactions to Jones's actions have varied from riots and murders in Afghanistan, and arrests in Florida on various charges, to death threats and bounties against him by some Muslim groups. Despite these threats, he continues on his crusade to burn Qurans and point out the threat that Islam poses to the West. Now, is fear of Islam what is motivating Jones? It doesn't seem so. Jones doesn't seem to be afraid of much. Then what is motivating him? If you listen to his words, you realize that he is convinced that Islam is of the devil and a danger to America, and that it is now and has always been a violent religion. So is Islamophobia the best way of characterizing Terry Jones's attitude toward Islam? I doubt it.

The term *Christophobia* (and its variant *Christianophobia*) is new, so new that many people have never heard of it although they are probably familiar with the sentiment that gives rise to it. According to the *Macmillan Dictionary* online, it means "intolerance of, hostility towards or discrimination against Christians"[7] (notice: no mention of "fear"). In his book *The Cube and the Cathedral*, George Weigel, an influential American Catholic, credits J. H. H. Weiler with coining the term. Weiler, an observant Jew, is an international legal scholar. He was looking for a term to describe the phenomenon he was seeing in much of Europe where even the mention of Christ or the church in public or private was sure to cut short any discussion.[8] Anti-Christian sentiment is not new, of course; what does appear new is the degree of it and the kind of places where it tends to show up.

The Middle East remains one of the most dangerous places for Christians to live. In Egypt, for example, Coptic Christians have often been the targets of persecution and discrimination since the overthrow of President Hosni Mubarak in 2011. With the beginning of the Iraqi War and the downfall of Saddam Hussein, hundreds of thousands of Christians have had to flee Iraq to escape persecution and death. In Europe, there is a rising tide of *Christophobia*. Since 1992, anti-Christian arsonists in Norway have burned down many churches. Christians in North America do not face the level of death threats, imprisonments, torture, and kidnappings as we see going on in Africa, China, and the Middle East. In the United States, the anti-Christian sentiments tend to be more political and ideological, although we have had our fair share of church burnings. In 2012, an organization known as American Atheists put up a billboard at Christmas in New York encouraging New Yorkers to "Keep the MERRY! Dump the MYTH!"

We have cited several examples of anti-Christian activities around the world; and this is just the tip of the proverbial iceberg. So what is motivating all these anti-Christian movements? Is it fear? Not likely. If you listen to the rhetoric of these groups, many have a visceral hatred of Christianity and the church. The reasons are as diverse as the attacks. So is Christophobia or Christianophobia the best way of characterizing these attitudes toward Christianity? I doubt it.

Now let's consider the terms again. People who disapprove of homosexuality are not "phobic" about it. They do not have panic attacks when they spot a lesbian couple. Their heart does not race when they encounter two men in intimate embrace. Most have a moral concern based in traditions which go back thousands of years. So what do we call that? I don't think we call that homophobia if we expect the conversation to take us anywhere productive.

Likewise, people who have a concern about global Islamic terrorism and Sharia law are not phobic about it. They do not break out in a sweat when they spot a Muslim. They do not run away from situations where they might meet a Muslim. They have a concern based on real events which have happened over the last thirty years, events which have been well documented and publicized on the news. So what do we call that? I don't think we call that Islamophobia if we expect to make any progress toward more peaceful and less fragmented society.

Finally, people who disagree with Christian teachings and practices are not phobic about it. They are not truly afraid of Christians. Adrenaline doesn't course through their veins whenever they have a close encounter with some Christian in a store; they do not roll up their sleeves and get ready to punch out a coworker when they spot a cross around her neck. They have a concern that Christianity has somehow damaged society and must be eliminated if culture is to progress. So what do we call that? I don't think we call it Christophobia if we hope to solve local and global problems in this century.

If we are to be slow to judge and agree that sometimes it is okay to listen, then we need new ways of expressing the differences that define us.

I recommend that we retire these terms altogether in favor of language that truly captures what people think and what they mean. Now, it won't be easy, because these words are such a regular part of our public conversation. You hear them on TV and the radio. You read them in newspapers and on blogs. Another reason it won't be easy is that they are quick and easy ways to prejudge, dismiss, and discriminate against people with whom we disagree.

If we are to be slow to judge and agree that sometimes it is okay to listen, then we need new ways of expressing the differences that define us.

Now, before you think I've gone off my rocker, consider what the Associated Press decided to do in 2012. Editors nixed words like *homophobia* and *Islamophobia* from their style books. AP writers are forbidden to use those words in their articles except when they are quoting another. According to AP Deputy Standards Editor Dave Minthorn, a phobia is an irrational, uncontrollable fear, often a form of a mental illness. Editors at AP decided that these words are not accurate and certainly not neutral. They prefer the use of a word like *anti-gay*. Words like *homophobia* and *Islamophobia*—which have become a staple in our public conversation—imply that those who reject homosexuality or have concerns about Islamic terror are mentally disturbed. Perhaps with the right medication or therapy or sensitivity training they could get over their "phobia."

Anti-gay may be slightly better, but it suffers the fate of all those *anti-* and *pro-* words in popular use. Is a person anti-abortion or pro-life? How the word is used will depend on which side of an issue the speakers are on. If a person is pro-choice (another interesting term; or are they pro-abortion?), then her opponent is anti-abortion. If a person is opposed to how abortion is practiced, then her ally in the struggle is pro-life. So *pro-* and *anti-* terms are politically charged and are used chiefly to prejudge and bludgeon political opponents and people with whom you disagree.

Without thinking about it, people tend to negatively construe words and phrases created with the "anti-" prefix—regardless of its application. At the same time, the masses prefer words and movements classified as "pro-" something. For example, the anti-abortion movement made great strides forward in the public when they rebranded themselves "pro-life." Going back a bit in history, it was the Federalists who won out over the anti-Federalists in the early days of America. It is always better, I suppose, to be perceived as *for* something rather than *against* it. The anti-death penalty crowd and the anti-gun movement may have important messages, but they will likely be lost in the rhetoric.

Another concern is this: if you say people are anti-gay, what exactly are they against? Are they opposed to the people whose orientation is different from their own? Or are they opposed to their sexual behavior? Or are they opposed to social and political policies which, from their perspectives, are dismantling cherished traditions and values?

Consider the same *anti-* with Islam. If people are anti-Islamic, what exactly are they against? Are they opposed to the people who practice the religion? Well, if so, we should probably call them anti-Muslim. Or are they opposed to the religion itself? Or are they opposed to certain acts attributed to those practicing the religion of Islam—in particular, acts of terror, (mis)treatment of women, (in)justices in Sharia law, etc.?

What about anti-Christian? I'm afraid that seems a bit too close to the word *anti-Christ*. If people are anti-Christian, what are they against? Like anti-Islamic are they opposed to the people who practice the religion, or are they opposed to the religion itself? It might be that they are opposed to what they perceive Christians and Christianity are doing to keep the world from progress.

Okay, let's say we agree in principle that the current language is not helpful in trying to develop kinder and gentler societies. In fact, if we're honest, I think we can say that the words themselves create a barrier against any opportunity we may have to achieve peaceful coexistence with people who think and act differently. Most people who use them do so to score points with their sympathizers. So what do we do now? What language are we going to use to replace it?

I must be honest to say that, when I began this chapter, I had hoped to come up with an alternative group of words that were more accurate and did not shut down the conversation. I would present these words in this book. I would convince everyone, and people all around the world would stop using hurtful, inaccurate words like *homophobia*, *Islamophobia*, and *Christophobia* and would instead use the words I had coined. Silly me!

Here is one list that I came up with: *homodissentic*, *Islamodissentic*, *Christodissentic*. (That's got a ring to it, don't you think?) The reason for choosing these words has to do with acknowledging that the real issue is not fear but disagreement, disapproval, and conflict. Some do not agree with homosexual practices as being good for individuals and good for society based on religious or nonreligious grounds. Others disapprove of what Islam teaches. They disagree that Islam deserves a place in Western society or that Islam is a peaceful religion, as its advocates insist. Still others oppose Christian teachings and practices; they criticize Christian leaders who think their ways are good for society. The Greek word for "disagree" is unwieldy (*apodokimazo*) and does not match well with the first part of each word: *homo-*, *Islamo-*, and *Christo-*.

If we turn to Latin, however, we find a word that has some resonance with English-speaking people and fits the first part of the word. The Latin word is *dissentire* (*dissentio*). The word means "to disagree with, to differ in opinion, to differ in one's feelings about, and to be in conflict over something." All of these meanings fit our current situation. In my view, *-dissentic* captures better what is going on in society than accusing others of being fearful or *-phobic* about something. As a Christian, I'm confident that people are not Christophobic as much as they are Christodissentic. Were I Muslim, I think I would see that others are not Islamophobic as much as they are Islamodissentic. Were I homosexual, I would understand that those who disagree with me are not homophobic as much as they are homodissentic.[9]

Now, I doubt that anyone will ditch *homophobic* for *homodissentic*, *Islamophobic* for *Islamodissentic*, or *Christophobic* for *Christodissentic*. I don't really expect them to. I just think it is important to raise the issue. The words we use matter. I do think it would benefit us all if those more inflammatory labels were retired completely in favor of more descriptive and honest language about what people think and stand for. In fact, I would propose that we refrain from using any labels at all when it comes to these deeply divisive issues; whatever labels we use to classify someone or summarize them can be turned to one party's advantage and another's disadvantage. Instead, we would be better off to commit ourselves to the hard work of truly listening to others, speaking truthfully about ourselves, and being slow to judge.

In the end, even after we have done the hard work of speaking and listening, we may not be convinced about another person's position. But that is not the point. It is not necessary that we all agree about every last thing. If I have learned anything from being on the radio for twelve years with Rabbi Federow and Father Arroyo, it is this: honest conversation may not end in agreement, but it will always end in clarity and friendship. The best we have to offer is to be generous with our time, loving in our actions, and tolerant in our demeanor. But honest dialogue is not easy; it is hard work, and few are willing to put in the hours and effort it takes. It is much easier to disrespect an opponent and be done with it. Labels can be useful; but in these cases, with so many emotions on the line, I doubt any label would or could work for long.

Undoubtedly, most people will continue to use *homophobic*, *Islamophobic*, and *Christophobic*, because these words do what they

> **Honest conversation may not end in agreement, but it will always end in clarity and friendship.**

want: they accuse and dismiss people with whom they disagree. By using them so cavalierly, people suggest, ever so subtly, that something is wrong with anyone who has a different perspective than they do. These terms play well to partisans, but I'm hoping that thoughtful people, who are more interested in shedding light than bringing heat, will see the wisdom of changing the tactless and inaccurate tags we place on people. If we want to be slow to judge and quick to listen, then, we need to retire these words completely.

With Paul let us pray that the Father would help us speak only those words that refresh and build up others.

QUESTIONS TO CONSIDER:

1. What do you think of the Associated Press's decision not to use words like *homophobia* and *Islamophobia* in their reports?

2. How do people react when they are called names like "bigot" or "Islamophobe" or some other name? Once those words are spoken, how can you keep the conversation going?

3. How should Paul's teaching on the kinds of words we use shape our conversations?

4. What is a better way to characterize the deep differences we see today between people?

THE PROBLEM WITH TOLERANCE

You hear a lot about "tolerance" these days. It has become a principle policy among Western democracies. Some consider it a public virtue, perhaps the highest virtue of all. Others, however, aren't so sure. The problem is not so much with the idea of tolerance but its practice. The way this kind of "tolerance" works is that some groups are to be tolerated, even celebrated, while others are to be condemned and marginalized for having done things, said things, or thought things which aren't part of the prevailing orthodoxy. Consider the story of Brendan Eich, the cofounder and short-term CEO of Mozilla. In 2008, he donated $1,000 to the campaign for Proposition 8, a California ballot initiative that set out to prohibit same-sex marriage. The initiative passed with 52 percent of Californians voting to affirm it. Six years later, in 2014, Eich was forced to step down from his position as CEO—a post he occupied only briefly—because stakeholders in his company objected to his donation—and apparently his politics—more than half a decade earlier. Now, at the time when Eich made the donation, presidential candidate Barack Obama publically claimed that he thought marriage should be between a man and a woman, too, agreeing with a majority of Americans. But in the last five years, the tide changed, President Obama changed in his thinking, and polls suggest that a majority of Americans are now in favor of same-sex marriages. This kind of tolerance—that is, tolerance toward a favored group and the ousting of those who express a contrary opinion—is in fact not a public virtue; it is a political strategy for centralizing power and shaping society.[1]

Now, Eich tried to make up for his "misstep" six years earlier by promising Mozilla employees that he would be actively pursuing equality, working with LGBT communities and their advocates to create a more welcoming environment, offering more inclusive health benefits, and strengthening antidiscrimination policies. Ironically, those who worked closest with him had no clue that he had made the donation, because he had never taken any action professionally which put people in same-sex relationships at any disadvantage. On a personal level, he promised to reach out to those who have felt marginalized and discover ways to help gay and lesbian employees of Mozilla understand their value to the company. But none of that mattered. Eich was forced to step down and the company issued an apology. Conor Friedersdorf, a well-known advocate for same-sex marriage, wrote this for *The Atlantic* (April 4, 2014): "Calls for his ouster were premised on the notion that all support for Proposition 8 was hateful, *and* that a CEO should be judged not just by his or her conduct in the professional realm, but also by political causes he or she supports as a private citizen."[2] Friedersdorf is worried that if this kind of thinking and behavior spreads, our society will be in real

Tolerance apparently means that it is okay to be intolerant to groups or people you despise.

trouble. I think Friedersdorf is right. It may be that we have already gone too far.

Andrew Sullivan, one of the country's best known and influential gay-rights advocates, also sees the danger inherent in this kind of intolerance. On his popular blog, "The Hounding of a Heretic," Sullivan wrote that Eich had been "scalped by some gay activists" after expressing his First Amendment rights and donating $1,000 to support Proposition 8. Sullivan wondered whether Eich would now be forced "to walk through the streets in shame" or be put in stocks.[3] It is important to notice that Sullivan refers dryly to Eich as a "heretic," implying, of course, that he has offended the prevailing orthodoxy. *Orthodoxy* is a term coined during centuries of religious controversies; it means "correct thinking" or "correct doctrine." In contrast, *heretics* are those who have the "wrong thinking" or "false doctrine." Over the last decade, the "correct" way to view same-sex relationships has changed, and Eich and people like him had better get with it or they will be shamed, shunned, and deprived of their livelihood. "The whole episode disgusts me," Sullivan writes, "as it should disgust anyone interested in a tolerant [there's that word again] and diverse society." He went on, "If we [the gay-rights movement today] are about intimidating the free speech of others, we are no better than the anti-gay bullies who came before us."[4] Sullivan was deluged with email responses by gay-rights activists accusing him of being on the wrong side of the issue. Tolerance apparently means that it is okay to be intolerant to groups or people you despise.

Sullivan is a wise fellow. He sees the danger of advocating for tolerance which moves in only one direction. For him, a truly tolerant society will welcome not only people of differing sexual orientations but people who think marriage should continue to be understood as a heterosexual union. How can we have that kind of society? Is it even possible for people with such fundamental differences to agree to disagree and then live and let live?

A BIT OF HISTORY

The whole notion of tolerance got its start among Western countries during the Enlightenment. It seemed to be a reasonable response to the religious and political wars which had devastated Europe during the sixteenth and seventeenth centuries; but this new tolerance was based upon an indifference to all values except political power and financial profitability. In his famous book *A Letter Concerning Toleration*, John Locke argued that the only reason to have a commonwealth in the first place is to provide people an opportunity to procure, preserve, and protect their civil interests. By civil interests he meant life, liberty, health, and the ability to acquire possessions such as money, land, houses, and furniture.[5] For Locke, this meant relegating our most important and enduring questions to private life. But A. J. Conyers is correct that private life was already out of reach of the government:

> In conceding the private realm to religion, the state was giving up its authority over what it never really governed anyway. Religion, on the other hand, was conceding to the state that over which it had always claimed to have some ultimate authority, for it had always claimed insight into the nature of a just society.[6]

So the state loses what it never had: control over people's private lives. The church, however, lost its place at the table and the influence that went with it. Religion, they say, is a private matter and you don't discuss it in public. At least, that is what I heard growing up. Anyone who thinks like that or curbs his or her behavior because of it is a child of the Enlightenment.

Since the seventeenth century, those in power celebrated tolerance as a public virtue. In the last decades of the twentieth century, tolerance/toleration has become entrenched as one of our principal virtues. Western democracies in particular have institutionalized it in a variety of ways. But we might well stop and ask: is tolerance a virtue at all? Consider for a moment some of the classical virtues: love, courage, moderation. By their very natures, virtues are always good and appropriate. There is no time when love is out of order. There is no situation when courage must be avoided. There is no day when moderation must be thrown out the window. But what of toleration? Aren't there limits to tolerance? Indeed, toleration is fundamentally different because everyone acknowledges that there must be limits to tolerance. We are not to tolerate anything and everything. For example, we should not be tolerant of people who get their kicks by mistreating animals, nor should we tolerate people who force sex on children. When John Locke wrote his famous *Letter Concerning Toleration*, he argued that tolerance had its limits. Some are not to be tolerated; for Locke, these included atheists and Roman Catholics. While no one today would agree with where Locke drew the line of toleration, everyone acknowledges that the line must be drawn somewhere. The problem, of course, is that no one agrees on where to draw the line. In the case above, the prevailing orthodoxy says we must allow same-sex marriages but not allow public dissent from anyone in a position of influence. But the winds of orthodoxy change; only ten years ago, the majority of Americans—including our 45th president—believed that marriage was between two persons of the opposite sex. When the Boniuk Institute for the Study and Advancement of Religious Tolerance at Rice University held its inaugural conference in 2005, they chose as their theme: "Tolerance and Its Limits."

Everyone acknowledges that the line must be drawn somewhere. The problem, of course, is that no one agrees on where to draw the line.

But again, when you think about it, a true virtue has no limits. A. J. Conyers wrote:

> A virtue strengthens our relationships. From a Christian perspective, all virtues serve the interests of love, love being the chief virtue and goal of life. Humility, patience, and prudence make it possible to love God, the world, and human beings, all in their proper order and proportion. Virtues are interconnected and, in a sense, all are one. They are themselves the goal of human life. We are created for this: to be capable of loving.[7]

So all virtues serve the greater good of love. There is never a time when love is out of place, unwanted, or unneeded. But everyone agrees that tolerance is sometimes out of place and to demonstrate tolerance in some situations is possibly even evil.

Now, if tolerance is not a virtue, what is it? Tolerance, in its current incarnation, has been turned into nothing less than a modern strategy to establish power, control society, and protect one's ability to prosper economically. Under the guise of tolerance, powerful movements within culture drive forward their agendas which elevate their friends and supporters; at the same time, they marginalize the voices of those who disagree for whatever reasons. While tolerance may depend on virtues such as humility, moderation, love, and patience, it is in fact a policy to achieve a particular end. If we are honest—and we should be—we must agree that the particular end which tolerance aims to achieve is itself good. Properly understood, tolerance aims to ease the tensions rooted in the significant differences facing a shrinking, global world; as such, it is not an end but a means to an end, a strategy that promotes harmony and peace with our common life. Some people have called this "peaceful coexistence." I would agree that, given all the stresses and fractures we have in the modern world, peaceful coexistence is something we must all work to achieve. But it will not be achieved by rolling over and playing dead or insisting that others do so.

As a student of Paul, I often find myself returning to his instruction to the Roman believers: "If it is within your power, make peace with all people" (Rom. 12:18). Paul does not regard peacemaking as an option; it is a command from the Lord's emissary to us. "Make peace." Peace must be *made*; it does not just happen. Tragedy happens. Chaos happens. Stuff happens, but not peace. Peace must be won and the battle will be long. Jesus said, "Blessed are the peacemakers—they will be called children of God" (Matt. 5:9). But there are limits to what you, I, or anyone else can do; so Paul qualifies it with "if it is within your power." You can't tell this from most English translations, but in the language of the New Testament the "your" is not "you" (singular) but "you" (plural). In other words, Paul isn't addressing the individual here; he is addressing the community. He is not saying that some individuals are to be the peacemakers and everyone else is allowed to be rabble-rousers. No, he is speaking to the entire church. The mission of God's people is to create and make peace. We may deputize certain gifted folk to take the lead, but the rest of us are obliged to follow. Still, some things are within our power; other things are not. We need to know the difference, and we need to understand when it is necessary to join forces with other like-minded peacemakers. But I think it is also true that we underestimate ourselves. We stop too soon. We come up short, in part because we are overwhelmed by the task ahead and lack confidence in ourselves. We also underestimate the power of the Spirit working in and through us. If we focus our attentions and efforts, if we pull together and not apart, then the Spirit can do more than we expected through us. But even then, that may not be enough, and Paul knows it. We cannot make peace with people who want us dead. We cannot make peace with those who will stop at nothing to defeat us. So there must be some impulse or incentive for our neighbor to end the hostility and live in harmony. Without that, I'm afraid a true and lasting peace can never be achieved.

At the close of the apostle's second letter to the Corinthians, he has a similar message, "Finally, brothers and sisters, keep rejoicing and repair whatever is broken. Encourage each other, think as one, and live at peace; and God, *the Author* of love and peace, will remain with you" (2 Cor. 13:11). The point is clear: when we can make a difference in creating peace, we must. I am just not sure that the modern strategy of tolerance advocated in secular democracies has a sufficient basis to create peace. If the tolerance shown to Brendan Eich is any indication, the edifice has already cracked and is about to crumble.

It is hard for my students to realize this, but the political entities we know as nation-states have not always been around. Pick up a world map and you see borders; they have not always been. Look at all the flags carried by athletes parading into Olympic stadium or waved at a World Cup soccer match; these colorful symbols of peoples and nations have not always engendered feelings of pride. Nations are a very recent development in world history, and the map is constantly changing.

When I was a child, one of my prize possessions was a steel globe. It was mounted on a steel base and tilted on its axis with a plastic arm. I loved that globe and spent hours playing with it and studying its features. I was fascinated with all the continents and oceans. Each country was identified by a different color. The locations of the largest cities were marked with either a dot or a small star, I can't remember which. At the equator there was a raised steel rim separating northern and southern hemispheres. One day, I took a little battery-operated motor, put a rubber wheel on it, and set it carefully on the top rim of the globe. The globe turned slowly (in the wrong direction!) for over an hour before the batteries played out. I turned out the light and set up a flashlight on one side to create night and day. I don't recall the date the globe was made, but it reflected the political realities of its day.

Today in my dining room I have another globe, a sixteen-inch library globe set into a wooden stand. Based on the geography, it must be at least fifty or sixty years old. As I compare it with a modern map, I see how many changes have come about in the last half century. Bech-uanaland is now Botswana. Rhodesia is now Zimbabwe. Formosa is now Taiwan. And the Union of Soviet Socialist Republics is now thirteen post-Soviet states with names like Armenia, Belarus, Kazakhstan, Georgia, Ukraine, Turkmenistan, and the Russian Federation. But even today the situation is still fluid; territories are being annexed and borders are changing. My point is that nations and states are a recent develop-ment; they have not always demanded our allegiance. They may seem rock solid and permanent, but they are as temporary as the Babylonian Empire.

Bureaucrats may wish it weren't so, but natural associations have the stronger claim on our lives and allegiances than government.

Now, before there were nations with flags and borders, human societies had been made up of people who belonged to a variety of "natural" associations usually based on ethnic, religious, family, and economic ties. Families, tribes, and communities of faith may be the best examples; but think, too, about organizations made up of people with common economic interests, such as shopkeepers, woodworkers, and other artisans. These associations, if they were large enough (for example, a tribal group), might have their own language, purposes, and goals, a shared sense of history, an agreed-upon authority structure, and some form of internal discipline to keep their members in line. This discipline typically took the form of honoring those who do right, according to community standards, and shaming those who do wrong. With the rise of the nation-states, however, the influence of natural associations began to give way to the more centralized authority of the state. As this happened, something else also happened: individuals became increasingly iso-lated. Competing interests meant that there were inevitable tensions between the organized state and these natural associations. Part of that comes from the fact that natural associations (family, faith community, friends, etc.) have a stronger hold on us. Governments collapse, borders change, and populations move, but natural associa-tions tend to go on. Now, natural associations might be disrupted for a time, but they generally survive. When Hurricane Katrina hit New Orleans in 2005, government programs and faith-based services had a difficult time keeping up with the chaos that followed. Families and friends were separated temporarily but later united in cities around the country like Houston and Atlanta. It took people months some-times to find their loved ones, but they didn't stop looking. Busi-nesses shut down temporarily in the flood-ravaged city only to open up again hundreds of miles away from the destruction. Bureaucrats may wish it weren't so, but natural associations have the stronger claim on our lives and allegiances than government.

Until the modern period, a person's identity had always been tied to a group. Sociologists refer to this dynamic as *dyadic personal-ity*. In other words, their identity and sense of self had been shaped by the group. They knew their place in the group. They knew who they were based on the history of the group. They knew what they believed based upon the values of the group. But now these groups were gone or at least marginalized; their authority and influence had been eclipsed by the larger, more powerful state. The result: confusion and isolation of the individual from all that gave his or her life meaning and purpose.

Now, the political leaders of these large nation-states decided that to protect the state, they must manage ethnic, tribal, and religious differences. It was in the interest of the state to make sure its citizens remained true to it and to downplay the influence of their former associations. Rather than viewing family, religious, ethnic, and economic ties as necessary and constructive aspects in the lives of people, state leaders began to promote the idea that these connections were voluntary and accidental. You were born into that clan by accident. Had you been born elsewhere, you would belong to a different family. If you want to stay true to it, then that is up to you. It is a private matter, not public. The main thing to remember is that you are a citizen of this country. That is where your allegiance should lie. Or you were born in that place so you are a Christian. Had you been born elsewhere, you might be a Muslim or a Hindu or nothing at all. If you want to stay true to your faith, then that is up to you. It is a private matter, not public. The most important thing is that you are a citizen of this country. This is where your allegiance should lie. More than anything else, the individual must see him- or herself as a citizen of the state; all other associations have to be overshadowed and eventually eclipsed by the power of the state. With these important personal matters stripped away or diminished, "the result was a powerful state and a lonely individual, two distinctive features of the modern period."[8]

While we tend to think of the world today almost exclusively in terms of large, diverse nation-states, this recent development has brought with it significant changes to our social, political, and religious lives. In the modern state, the centralization of the government depends largely on making sure our public life is secular and not religious. As Michael Walzer noted, in order to establish peace, differences must be managed.[9] But who is going to do the managing? That matters, as you might imagine. Generally, they are managed by a single, dominant group in the country that organizes public life in such a way as to reflect and maintain its own values. In other words, these managers must protect their positions of power and make sure their livelihoods are not endangered. Unmanaged differences are sure to "disturb the peace." Religious differences—because they make ultimate claims—must be managed above all. So there are three options:

1. insist that everyone practice the same religion;

2. forbid religion from entering the public square at all; or

3. consign religion to the private sphere.

Now, no one I know in America has suggested option 1 with a straight face. There are constitutional restrictions against establishing a state religion in America. Private citizens and voluntary associations may band together and advocate that everyone be Christians or Muslims; but the government is prohibited from getting into that act by the First Amendment. Generally, it is options 2 and 3 which have characterized Western democracies. In France and Turkey, the practice of laicism has effectively excluded religion from public life (option 2). In the United States and other Western democracies, freedom of religion may be guaranteed, but there are enough social and legal rules in place to consign religion effectively to the margins (option 3). One may be guaranteed freedom of worship—no mayor or governor or civil servant is going to prohibit you from going to the church you choose on a Sunday. On the other hand, you may not be free to practice your religion the rest of the week by the way you run your business or conduct your personal affairs if your beliefs run counter to the policies of the state or do not fit in with the prevailing orthodoxy. Some people in America have described it this way: in America, we have freedom of worship but not freedom of religion. If worship is limited to what you do in private, fine. If religion seeks a place of influence in the public square, then it's not so fine.

There can be no doubt that the religious wars that ravaged Europe in the sixteenth and seventeenth centuries played a significant role in how modern philosophers and statesmen have constructed their views of tolerance. But the annexation of land, the rise of powerful nation-states, and the growth of trade with its promises to make some wealthy made Europe ripe for conflict even without the stresses and strains caused by religious differences. In other words, religion was not the only factor leading to the horrors of the Thirty Years War; but it was partly to blame.

TOLERANCE VERSUS FAITH

I agree with Conyers that the modern doctrine of toleration has failed to bring us peace and will continue to fail as long as it splits life into public and private spheres and assigns questions of ultimate concern to a role only on the margins. As I have written elsewhere, the line of separation (between church and state) does not run neatly through a person's soul. When a man votes, his faith will inform his vote. It is not a matter of "should" but a matter of "will." When a woman takes the oath of office, she cannot lay aside her religious convictions; they will inform how she sees the world and how she leads. Political leaders can say they will try not to let their religion "interfere" with their duties, but again: how do you isolate one part of a person from another? How do you separate fragrance from perfume? How do you detach thought from mind?

While the modern doctrine of tolerance pretends initially to support the idea of religion, it will almost immediately neutralize any sincere expressions of religious conviction if such expressions disagree with the majority in power. With the one hand, the tolerant democracy gives—and it can afford to give because it is a powerful, prosperous state with seemingly unlimited resources—with the other it takes away. When the doctrine of tolerance is wed with political power, then tolerance will give way to other kinds of intolerance.[10]

This was clearly evident to what happened to Phil Robertson, the patriarch to the Robertson family and star of the hit TV show *Duck Dynasty*. In late 2013, he was suspended by A&E for what he said in an interview with *GQ* magazine. After being asked his views about what is sinful, Robertson responded, "Start with homosexual behavior and just morph out from there. Bestiality, sleeping around with this woman and that woman and that woman and those men."

Then, to show he wasn't just making this up, he paraphrased 1 Corinthians 6:9–10: "Don't be deceived. Neither the adulterers, the idolaters, the male prostitutes, the homosexual offenders, the greedy, the drunkards, the slanderers, the swindlers—they won't inherit the kingdom of God. Don't deceive yourself. It's not right."[11]

Robertson was merely expressing what Christians have taught for two thousand years about right and wrong. But the people who run A&E were not pleased with Robertson's response. In their official statement to the media, they said, "His personal views in no way reflect those of the A&E Networks, who have always been strong supporters and champions of the LGBT community."[12]

Philosopher Jerry Walls observed, "It is perfectly fine to be a 'strong supporter' of a behavior that traditional religious believers have held to be sinful for millennia. One can express this view forthrightly and with conviction, with no fear of reprisal or negative consequences. But if you affirm traditional Christian morality, you will be silenced, suspended, forced to apologize and perhaps lose your job."[13] Walls refers to what happened to Robertson as "the latest high profile instance of the ironic phenomenon of left wing fundamentalism in the guise of tolerance." The irony, of course, lies in the fact that "fundamentalist" Christians are consistently ridiculed for being judgmental and narrow-minded and forcing their views on others. Now those on the left who detest fundamentalist Christians are adopting those very ways. Why? Because they are in positions of power and can do so.

I think you can see that there are problems-a-plenty with tolerance as it is currently practiced in our culture. There is, however, an authentic version of tolerance with roots deep in the Christian faith which can help us rediscover kingdom priorities for this world. We turn our attentions to that in the next chapter.

With Jesus let us ask the Father to bring in His kingdom and let His will be done on earth as it is in heaven.

QUESTIONS TO CONSIDER:

1. If tolerance is not a virtue, what exactly is it?

2. What can churches do to make peace with all people whenever it is in their power? What stops us from taking Paul seriously on this straightforward directive?

3. Where should Christians draw the line when it comes to toleration? What should believers do when other Christians draw the line in a different place?

4. Under what circumstances is it likely that "tolerance" will slip into "intolerance"?

AUTHENTIC TOLERANCE

Let's begin thinking about an authentic version of tolerance rather than the kind of pseudo-tolerance we see in practice across our society. Is it possible to have a society where authentic tolerance exists? Well first, let's consider what the word *tolerance* means. Merriam-Webster online offers several definitions, but here are the two entries most relevant: "1. Capacity to endure pain or hardship; 2a. sympathy or indulgence for beliefs or practices differing from or conflicting with one's own; 2b. the act of allowing something."[1]

First of all, notice that tolerance means enduring something or allowing something which causes you discomfort, hardship, and pain. In other words, you cannot tolerate something which does not make you uncomfortable. If you are in favor of same-sex marriage or have no problem with it, you cannot claim to be tolerant of same-sex relationships because they do not make you uncomfortable. You can only be tolerant of beliefs and practices that make you uncomfortable. So in this case, tolerance means putting up with people who claim that marriage must be between a man and a woman. If you legally carry a concealed handgun, you cannot claim to be tolerant of those who advocate Second Amendment rights, because they do not make you uncomfortable. You can only be tolerant of beliefs and practices contrary to your own. In this case, tolerance means putting up with people who think gun violence can be stopped only by strin-gent gun control.

Let's consider it this way: In Houston, people can be said to tolerate the heat and the humidity because the weather makes them so uncomfortable. No one would say they tolerate a spring day in the 70s with low humidity. In Edmonton, Alberta, residents tolerate the cold in the winter and mosquitoes in the summer because the temperatures can be dangerously cold and the mosquitoes a real nuisance. No one there would say they tolerate a mosquito-free, warm spring day in central Canada. The bottom line is this: without discomfort and fundamental disagreement, there can be no such thing as tolerance.

For decades, I've been around interfaith dialogue meetings. Often, these meetings are little more than sharing all the ways our religions are the same. Now, to be honest, there are many similarities between the world's great religions. We need to know those things and celebrate them. But—and this is a big *but*—there are also many signifi-cant differences between the world's religions. If all we do is talk about the sameness, then we never get to tolerance. I often have said at meetings like this, until there is some discom-fort around the room, until someone gets hot under the collar, we're not going to accomplish much in terms of true, authentic dialogue.

> **The bottom line is this: without discomfort and fundamental disagreement, there can be no such thing as tolerance.**

We must grapple with and be honest with all the ways our religions differ. That will challenge and offend us, but it will give us a chance to demonstrate authentic tolerance.

Now, speaking of offense, we live in a day when everyone (it seems) is offended by something. In the past, if people were offended, they kept it to themselves. Apparently, they thought they lived in a sort of world where challenges to their beliefs and practices did not or should not happen. Today, it doesn't take much for a person to declare their outrage over a particular offense. Think about how often people claim they have been offended and demand that someone (usually someone in government) do something about it. Where is the tolerance in that? We do not have the right to never be offended. We do not have the right to hear only words we want to hear or see only signs we want to see. We often hear of people going to court because they've been offended. I can only be offended if I somehow believe I have the right not to be. An unintended consequence of all our sensitivity training and intercultural exchange has been an entitlement mentality, "I have the right not to be offended. You went to the training. You sat through the seminar. You know you're not supposed to talk like that, act like that, or even think like that." Mandatory training seldom gets us where we want to be. If I understand that this world consists of people with different beliefs, values, and practices, and some of those beliefs, values, and practices are going to rub me the wrong way, then I can begin to develop genuine tolerance, a "live and let live" mentality. If, however, I insist that everyone speak, act, and think in ways that do not make me feel uncomfortable, that is not tolerance; that is tyranny of the one.

Now, this is not to say that we must tolerate everything. Some things are so offensive and injurious to others that they should not be allowed. Human trafficking comes to mind because, as I write this, Boko Haram, an Islamic terror group in Nigeria, has taken 270 schoolgirls captive and is selling them into marriages to militants. Some things are worthy of our outrage and immediate action. Genocide and crimes against humanity must be resisted with every fiber of our being. To do nothing about it when we are able would be an offense against God and humanity.

RECLAIMING AUTHENTIC TOLERANCE

Since the modern project of tolerance will likely fail, it is important for believers to reclaim an authentic practice of tolerance in order to repair the fractures which are becoming more apparent in our shrinking, global world. My point here is to say that authentic tolerance can only come from inside religion, not by setting it aside for a more neutral stance, which is not so neutral after all. I call this authentic tolerance because it can lead to authentic existence for any who practice it. Authentic tolerance is an entirely natural human enterprise because it will deal at some point with ultimate questions that all people ask, questions of meaning and purpose:

- Who are we?
- Where have we come from?
- Where are we going?
- Is there anything worth living for? dying for?
- Is there a purpose to my being here?

The modern strategy of tolerance has merely postponed these kinds of questions in order to deal with more manageable problems. In fact, according to many moderns and post-moderns, these ultimate questions cannot be answered finally, so why should we try in the first place?

For tolerance to be authentic, it must be disentangled from any sort of alliance it has with power and material wealth. People in power will be tempted to impose their brand of tolerance and uniformity of thought and action on others, which is the most intolerant thing they could do. Again, tolerance depends on being willing to endure hardship and discomfort; it often means allowing words, thoughts, and actions with which we disagree. On the other hand, the modern strategy of tolerance has been all about managing language, preserving and protecting the power of a few, and maintaining their values.

Let me identify two of my major assumptions. First, everyone is interested in "the good life," at least for themselves. Those with a bit of altruism running in their veins may wish that their neighbors, friends, and people like them could experience "the good life" too. Furthermore, I think most people want to live in a "good" society. The problem comes in how you define "the good." Thinking politically, Democrats in America have a sense of what the good life and good society are. They enact policies and pursue legislation consistent with their idea of "the good." Likewise, Republicans in America believe they know what a good life and a good society are. They use their political positions to gain favor with the electorate to win elections so they can pursue "the good," as well. But their ideas are often at odds with the Democrats across the aisle. No one is seeking to destroy America, despite what some pundits would have you believe. The issue is that Republican and Democratic ideas about "the good" differ so significantly. My point is that everyone is seeking "the common good," but with all the differences standing in the way (politically, religiously, ethnically, etc.), the path forward will demand the kind of authentic tolerance I'm trying to describe. I do believe there is a practice of tolerance which is not based on indifference to the notion of "the good." Likewise, I do think there is an authentic tolerance we can discover which does not privilege power and material wealth over deeper, more abiding questions.

Theologian A. J. Conyers argues that the central mystery of the incarnation, or what he calls "the powerful fact of the incarnation," provides a sufficient basis to reorder our lives toward "the good" and establish peace where there are so many differences.[2] Now, we must quickly point out that Conyers is not talking about "the doctrine of the incarnation." By their very nature, doctrines must be worked out over time by philosophers and theologians. They are subject to being believed or not believed based on how the doctrine is expressed. Conyers is speaking about the central conviction that God has become flesh in the particular person of history whom we know as Jesus of Nazareth. To put it in Paul's language, "God was in Christ reconciling the world" (2 Cor. 5:19 NKJV). The point I wish to make here is that the incarnation as an event in history takes precedence over any sense of doctrinal explanation or understanding.

> The incarnation as an event in history takes precedence over any sense of doctrinal explanation or understanding.

As a "fact" or "conviction" rather than a doctrine, it is not necessary that we grasp the reality of the incarnation and express it in some systematic fashion on a theology exam. It is more important that the reality grasps us and reorients our lives essentially toward a more tolerant and open attitude toward others who happen to share our same enfleshed existence. For most Christians, the incarnation is a mystery which we can never fully explain. How God became flesh and dwelt among us is just beyond us. But the fact that He did ought to inspire us.

The incarnation becomes the basis for hope, for it was God who made the first move to address our dire situation. If our lives are shaped by the vigorous conviction that in Christ God has become flesh and lived among us, then even though the world is filled with suffering (because of intolerance and other problems), we realize that suffering does not have the last word, nor are we beyond hope. Since God has entered our world, with all of its differences and discomforts (John 1:1–18), then our world must be good and our future hopeful. This approach to life stands in sharp distinction to the modern notion that the world is to be feared, subdued, and made safe for power and profit for a few. Or as Thomas Hobbes put it: life is "solitary, poor, nasty, brutish, and short."[3]

If the fact of the incarnation offers us hope, then the purpose of the incarnation provides reconciliation. Initially, this means reconciliation between God and humanity; but by extension, it means reconciliation between people of all types, especially those who find differences hard to tolerate and those who imagine that the barriers separating us are insurmountable. In practice, reconciliation looks a lot like tolerance and demands that we truly listen to others. Reconciliation can only be realized when we practice an open heart in what many will regard as risky situations.

Despite the fact that some people try to use religion to promote intolerance and violence, I believe the church, the body of Christ, is the right culture for reclaiming an authentic practice of tolerance. If "God was in Christ reconciling the world" (2 Cor. 5:19 NKJV), then the reconciliation of "all things" becomes the primary mission of the church. According to Scripture, the reconciliation of "all things" has already begun in the resurrection of Jesus (Easter) and the birth of the church (Pentecost). The church, then, is the first part of the world to be reconciled to God (Col. 1:15–20); now the rest is sure to follow. Our mission is to take that reconciliation to the ends of the earth and make it available to all people. In Christ, God loved the world. We, as members of His body, are part of that world and so are all the others who are very different from us. When you look at it this way, the incarnation, and the reconciliation it calls for, mean that all things and all people are ultimately interconnected.

Now, I am writing this book as a member of the Baptist denomination in the U.S.A. Baptists are not typically associated with tolerance, but they are associated with strong convictions, passion, and fervency in faith. Still, despite popular perceptions, there is a significant tradition of tolerance and freedom of conscience within many Baptist thinkers, beginning with Thomas Helwys, one of our earliest Baptist theologians. Although Baptists make up the largest Protestant denomination in America today, our numbers were slight at the turn of the seventeenth century. Baptists were a religious minority that faced hostility from both established churches and government officials. In the face of persecution, Baptists advocated religious liberty, initially for themselves but, by extension, for all. They formulated the doctrine directly from the Christian Scriptures, reason, and human experience. Essentially, they argued that governments should not meddle in matters of religion and conscience. Had they known it, they would have agreed with the Quranic injunction that there is no compulsion in religion (2:256). Baptist leaders scandalized some people at the time by advocating religious liberty for Roman Catholics, Turks, Jews, and heretics alike.[4] Religious uniformity, they believed, was not necessary to ensure the domestic tranquility.

The incarnation reveals something else we did not know about God and humanity. Consider this early Christian hymn found in Paul's letter to the Philippians:

In other words, adopt the mind-set of Jesus the Anointed. *Live with His attitude in your hearts. Remember:*

Though He was in the form of God,
> He chose not to cling to equality with God;

But He poured Himself out *to fill a vessel brand new;*
> a servant in form
> and a man indeed.

The very likeness of humanity,
He humbled Himself,
> obedient to death—
> a merciless death on the cross!

So God raised Him up to the highest place
> and gave Him the name above all.

So when His name is called,
> every knee will bow,
> in heaven, on earth, and below.

And every tongue will confess
> "Jesus, the Anointed One, is Lord,"
> to the glory of God our Father! (Phil. 2:5–11)

When Jesus emptied Himself and died a merciless death on the cross, He left behind a "lordly example" of humility and called us to imitate it.[5] If we take this call seriously, then we are to live according to the kind of radical humility we see demonstrated in Jesus' lowly actions. One way this will manifest itself is in a willingness to listen to others. This does not mean listening in order to gain an advantage or simply to seek knowledge that we can use against another. No, it means listening expecting to hear something of value, expecting to hear the truth.

A. J. Conyers surveyed the biblical evidence regarding tolerance and defines it as "a willingness to hear other traditions and learn from them."[6] We will explore some examples of this in a moment. For now, I think it safe to say that, if we are to see authentic tolerance exist and flourish in our time, we will need a good dose of humility inspired by the example of Jesus. This kind of authentic tolerance reflects a depth to humility that we do not often see in the world; it is a willingness to set aside our own agendas to attend to the voice of the other. Humility, then, is what will make true dialogue possible. Any kind of dialogue that is birthed in authentic tolerance will not be content to talk about how similar we are, how much we agree, and the like; it may begin with what we have in common, but it will not stop until we have engaged our most cherished and deeply held beliefs. It will not shrink back when we uncover the depth of differences between us. This kind of dialogue stands in sharp relief to the pseudo-toleration that makes dialogue contingent on following preset rules that predetermine the result. Conyers went on to say:

> Just as pseudo-toleration answers power with power, it answers bigotry with bigotry. The hallmark of authentic tolerant practice should be the listening heart for which the wise king prayed and not the management of language and appointing itself the arbiter of all public discussions.[7]

So we are back once again to Solomon the wise king who prayed for a "listening heart" in order to rule well over God's people Israel.

Another way of envisioning authentic tolerance is to practice an open heart, the kind of open heart we see in hospitality. This means welcoming strangers and serving their physical, social, and spiritual needs. In any kind of cross-cultural exchange, both parties are strangers or aliens to each other. So hospitality involves not only giving but also receiving in a way that gives dignity and honor to the other. Amy Oden has written, "Acts of inclusion and respect, however small, can powerfully reframe social relations and engender welcome."[8]

There is a sense in which the authentic tolerance we have been describing here is nothing new. It is actually the recovery of a practice and disposition that the church had in its early centuries before

Christianity became the dominant religion of the West. Even after the Constantinian revolution (fourth century AD), some Christian writers displayed an open disposition to the truth, beauty, and goodness found in other cultures and religions. Now, we must admit that tolerance and openness were not practiced by everyone everywhere, but they were practiced by some of the church's greatest leaders at seminal moments in the church's history. These leaders genuinely listened to other traditions and were open to learn from them. For example, Paul memorized some of the lines of pagan Greek poetry and admired the Athenians for their religiosity (Acts 17). Justin Martyr (d. 165) associated the *Logos* of Greek philosophy with Christ and made possible a link from the earliest, pre-Christian philosophers to Christian theology. Likewise, Clement of Alexandria (d. 215) incorporated some of the best of Greek literature and philosophy into his own writings. Although he quoted pagan writers nearly three hundred times, for him Scripture remained supreme. For Clement, the apostle John was not in competition with Homer or any other philosopher. Still, if the Greeks expressed anything that is true in their books or philosophy, would it have been by chance or by Providence? Clement would clearly say, "Providence" (*Stromata* 1.94). Similarly, Augustine (AD 354–430) affirmed that wherever truth was found, it belonged to the Master (*De Doctrina* 2.28). On the question of truth, Thomas Aquinas (AD 1225–1274) draws from Christian, Jewish, Muslim, and pagan authors, recognizing that, if truth is real, it must be real for everyone (*Summa Theologiae, primar pars.* Q16 "On Truth"). For Aquinas, if any culture or religion has been enlightened by truth, it can be no other than the truth revealed by the One God, the Father of our Lord Jesus Christ. This is a far cry from modern expressions of relativism: "what is true for me is not necessarily what is true for you." On the contrary, in the practice of authentic tolerance, there is a pressing forward to an idea of truth that is common for everyone because it is real for everyone.[9] When we come to the modern period, C. S. Lewis read the great Norse and Greek myths and found in them a prefiguration of truths revealed through Christ. We will have more to say about Lewis in a later chapter.

But it was not just the occasional Christian theologian and writer who paid attention and drew from non-Christian sources; consider how Christians expressed their faith in other ways. The Gospels, for example, were not a new genre of literature such as the world had never seen before. When Matthew, Mark, Luke, and John decided to commit their accounts of the life of Jesus to writing, they looked about and found a suitable vehicle. The New Testament Gospels are a type of ancient biography common in the ancient world. Plenty of parallels between the Gospels and ancient biographies exist from that era, including Plutarch's *Lives* and Suetonius' *The Lives of the Caesars*. Certain features and interests characterize ancient biographies that are not found in their modern counterparts. The Gospels follow well the pattern of these ancient biographies. Their subject matter, Jesus of Nazareth, is of course unique, but Christians apparently had no qualms about using a literary form which outsiders also used to celebrate the lives and examples of their chief citizens.

As part of his missionary strategy, the emissary Paul kept in touch with his churches by writing letters. But Paul didn't invent letters or the letter format. No, he wrote his letters following closely the way Jews, Greeks, and Romans wrote their letters in the ancient world. He even used secretaries to help him write his letters just like Cicero and other famous, ancient letter writers.[10] Paul had some unique features in his letters; for example, he altered the stereotypical greeting found in nearly all ancient letters to read, "Grace and peace be with you from God our Father and the Lord Jesus the Anointed" (Phil. 1:2). Again, Paul's subjects are unique, but he had no problem with making use of a well-known literary form to keep in touch with the churches.

Not only did the earliest followers of Jesus adopt literary conventions employed commonly among outsiders, they also made use of their material culture, as well. While Jews had a unique relationship to the scroll form of a book, as far back as the second century AD there is evidence that Christians preferred the codex form, that is, the form of a book we use today.[11] Although it is unlikely that Christians invented the codex, they borrowed it and made ample use of it in making copies of their most important manuscripts, such as the books of the New Testament.

And what about Christian worship? There is considerable evidence from the ancient world that pagans approached their gods in prayer by raising their hands above their heads, much as we see Christians doing in Pentecostal and evangelical churches today. Jews, too, raised their hands as they approached the One, True God in worship at the synagogue and at the temple in Jerusalem. Who started this prayer posture and why is unclear, but

Paul's subjects are unique, but he had no problem with making use of a well-known literary form to keep it in touch with the churches.

it is not surprising that early Christians adopted it and also raised their hands in prayers to God the Father. We read descriptions of this prayer posture known as the *orans* in early Christian literature. Images of it are still visible in catacomb paintings in Rome. Although Christians adopted this pagan and Jewish practice as part of their worship, many decided to alter it to reflect something unique about their theology. Rather than raising their hands high above their heads, they brought their hands down until their bodies resembled the form of a cross. In other words, when Christians made the sign of the cross in those days, they did so with their entire bodies. We read about accounts of some people who were baptized as they made the sign of the cross. We know that others went to their martyrdom standing erect with arms outstretched in imitation of the cross.[12]

Moving to the world of Christian art, we have all seen Christian mosaics or art featuring holy figures with halos behind their heads. Where did this image come from? Well, again, Christians did not create it; they borrowed it. It appeared earlier in Egyptian, Greek, and Roman art, perhaps as a representation of the disc of the sun. The halo was adopted by early Christians sometime in the fourth century AD, appearing on icons and in later art. One of the first figures to have a halo was Christ. In a way, this makes perfect sense. If Jesus is the Light of the World and God created the sun to bring light to the world, then linking the Light of the World with the sun unites the physical and spiritual spheres. Representing the Light of the World, by the light of the sun behind His head, fits perfectly within the art forms and cultural sensibilities of the age. In later Christian art, halos figure prominently on the heads of other holy people, such as Joseph, Mary, and the apostles because of their close association with Jesus. But again we see something unique happen in Christian art history. In some paintings and icons from the Middle Ages, the halo includes an image of the cross radiating from the head of the saint who is being depicted. This innovation is distinctly Christian, even if the form of the halo goes back centuries to other cultures.[13]

For the first three centuries, Christians did not gather in buildings specially constructed for that purpose. Initially, they met in the homes of some of the wealthier members, as Paul describes in 1 Corinthians 16:19: "The churches in Asia salute you. Aquila and Prisca send a heartfelt greeting in the Lord along with those who gather at their house." There is also good evidence that Jesus' followers continued to gather at the Jerusalem temple until it was destroyed in

AD 70. Away from the holy city, they often worshiped side-by-side with Jews in their synagogues. When they did begin constructing buildings in the fourth century AD, they did not model their sacred spaces on Roman temples. Instead, they found a suitable form in the Roman basilica. The Romans used their basilicas for public meetings, large markets, and courts of law because they could accommodate a large crowd. Christians borrowed the basilica form from the Romans, with its large open spaces and vaulted ceilings. There was nothing particularly innovative or Christian in the earliest churches until they decided to construct them in a cruciform pattern typical of the footprint of cathedrals you can see today in Europe. Once again, Christians had no qualms about looking into their broader cultures, adopting what they found there, and eventually adapting it to their unique needs.

Now, we could continue to cite examples where Christians found something valuable and useful in the "pagan" literature, ideas, practices, art, and architecture and put it to good use to reflect their own piety. This is more than utilitarianism or a refusal to "reinvent the wheel." They adopted—and in many cases adapted—these ideas, literary forms, scribal practices, worship postures, and artistic representations because they found in them something of utility, value, and beauty. Even if they could not contain the whole truth as found in Christianity, they prefigured that truth, since those who created them were themselves created in God's glorious image. This does not mean, of course, that Christians adopted anything and everything without discrimination. No, they were wise in their appropriation of the arts and ideas from their non-Christian neighbors. They weighed these matters carefully and borrowed what they could. It is clear from their writings that church leaders rejected ideas which they considered incompatible with the central message of the gospel. But their willingness to appropriate so much from others demonstrates a level of tolerance, listening, and openness rarely seen in recent centuries. But seldom did they borrow anything without adapting it and reshaping it over time to reflect their unique views of God, the world, and humanity. In a sense, we can say that they took the best that culture had to offer and baptized it in the name of the Father, Son, and Holy Spirit to make it useful for kingdom purposes.

We've witnessed a related phenomenon over the last fifty years. If you were to climb into a time machine and transport yourself back to the 1950s as Michael J. Fox did in the movie *Back to the Future*, you would understand better what church life was like in those days. Walk into your average Protestant church and you'd see two musical instruments—for those churches which allowed such things: an organ on one side of the pulpit, a piano on the other. In the 1960s, when the Jesus movement began to sweep across the nation, a lot of the music heard in churches began to change. Slowly—and I mean slowly—drums, acoustic and electric guitars, synthesizers, and other instruments appeared on the platform next to the pulpit. At first, there was pushback from members who preferred Bach to rock, but eventually the kind of music heard on top-forty stations around the country replaced anthems, chorales, and organ preludes in many churches. I'll let a bona fide musicologist assess the significance of these changes, but I was on the ground in the 1970s playing "Jesus music" in churches, theaters, coffee houses, and high school football stadiums. The root of contemporary Christian music—which is the preferred term today—was in the "Jesus music" of the 1960s and 70s. "Jesus music" originated on the West Coast among musicians who were converted to Christianity in churches like Calvary Chapel

> [Christians] were wise in their appropriation of the arts and ideas from their non-Christian neighbors.

in Costa Mesa, California. These born-again musicians continued to play the same styles of music they knew and loved. The beat and melodies may have been top-forty folk or rock-and-roll, but the message in the lyrics was distinctly Christian. The music caught on and quickly spread east. Because the music performed by Love Song, Larry Norman, Dove, The Pat Terry Group, Phil Keaggy, Petra, and many other groups sounded similar to contemporary rock and folk music, conservative leaders criticized the movement as worldly and demonic. I recall sitting through a Basic Youth Conflicts Seminar with Bill Gothard in Oklahoma City as he claimed the beat of rock-and-roll and Jesus music had their roots in African religion and must be avoided at all costs. The title to Larry Norman's 1972 song sums up the spirit of the movement: "Why Should the Devil Have All the Good Music?" The point, I hope, should be obvious: even though there was some initial opposition, the worship of the church today has been shaped heavily by rock-and-roll, folk, country, bluegrass, and other music styles. These styles originated outside the church but were appropriated by believers in order to express their essential message in relevant ways to new audiences.

In the early days of our radio show, we'd begin the first hour with a twenty- to thirty-second segment of some contemporary rock song, and the rabbi—we referred to him as "the rock-and-roll rabbi"—would take a minute to lay out the theology which floated just below the surface of the melody and the lyrics. I was often amazed at how he was able to get to the heart of a song and figure out a relevant message steeped in his Jewish theology. To be clear, these were not religious songs in the slightest, but the rabbi was able to hear in their lyrics a core message which expressed the frailty of humankind and our longing for redemption.

Authentic tolerance seeks to listen to others, not because it expects to hear the whole truth, but because the whole truth is yearned for, desired, and reflected in part through the goodness of God's image in people who come at life quite differently than we do. They may be Muslims, Hindus, Sikhs, or just old rock-and-rollers. They may be Democrats, Republicans, gay-rights activists, or Baptist professors. If we will attune ourselves to their voices, we may hear something worth hearing and knowing.

Authentic tolerance will be quick to listen and slow to speak, as James instructed his scattered churches. But the practice of authentic tolerance will also put up with and bear up against ideas, values, and practices which are remote and strange by our own standards. Recall the counsel of Paul in Colossians 3:12–14:

> [12] Since you are all set apart by God, made holy and dearly loved, clothe yourselves with *a holy way of life*: compassion, kindness, humility, gentleness, and patience. [13] Put up with one another. Forgive. Pardon any offenses against one another, as the Lord has pardoned you, because you should act in kind. [14] But above all these, put on love! Love is the perfect tie to bind these together.

As the temperature in the room rises, as blood pressures go up, as past offenses are recalled, authentic tolerance is committed to staying at the table until forgiveness is achieved and differences are at least talked through, if not resolved. The qualities that we will need to live out a more authentic version of tolerance are found in this passage: compassion, kindness, humility, gentleness, patience, and, above all, love. If we achieve anything near an authentic version of tolerance as we've described here, I'm convinced that we will reach détente with non-believers, and we will also deepen and widen our Christian faith. We will be able to stand up for Jesus, bear witness to our faith, defend it against attack, and yet do so in a way which is slow to judge and quick to listen.

With Paul let us pray that the Father will help us wrap ourselves in compassion, humility, gentleness, and patience.

QUESTIONS TO CONSIDER:

1. Why do people today think they have a right not to be offended?

2. How does a doctrine differ from a conviction?

3. If Jesus is the lordly example of humility, what does that mean for the kinds of conversations we have with people who look, think, and act differently?

4. During the last year who has sat at your kitchen table? What would it take to open up your home and hearth to people of other faiths? What would it mean for the world if Christians around the world showed hospitality to those outside the faith?

LISTENING TO A MUSLIM LEADER:
FETHULLAH GÜLEN

> "A heart makes a good home for a friend."
>
> —Yunus Emre (1240?–1320?)

The subtitle to this book, *Sometimes It's OK to Listen*, may need a bit of explanation. Notice that I didn't say it is always okay to listen. Nor did I say that there is a moral mandate to always listen. It is "sometimes" okay to listen. Why do I say that? There are some ideas that are not worth your time and certain people to whom you need not listen. It takes wisdom to know the difference. That is why we began talking about wisdom.

If a person insists on speaking and begins to rant about the inferiority of certain races, that person may be heard, but we can and should reject their ideas. In America, all people are guaranteed by our Constitution the right of free speech, but not the right to be heard and taken seriously. As a courtesy, we may choose to give them a platform to address others, but we don't have to entertain their ideas for more than half a second. Likewise, if people in Pakistan condemn the Ahmaddiya Muslims as un-Islamic because they do not agree with certain mainstream Muslim teachings, those people should not be heard. They may have the right in certain countries to express their views or to turn their views into laws, but they do not have the right to be taken seriously anywhere else in the world. My point is: it is not always okay to listen to toxic ideas, for their only effect is to lay waste to lives and communities. I wish I could say that such ideas are rare in the world, but they are not. Every idea must be judged on its merits. Every proposal must be judged by what it produces. That takes time. That takes humility. That takes wisdom.

I can hear someone say, "You're right. I'm not going to listen to those Democrats. They're way too liberal for my tastes." Another will say, "I agree, that's why I don't listen to any Republicans. Look at what they are trying to do to our country." Yet another will say, "I'm with you. I don't trust Muslims. Whenever they open their mouths, I know they're lying." No, that is not what I'm saying. "Toxic ideas" are not simply those ideas that you find disagreeable or hard to swallow. Often, the people we must learn to tolerate and listen to most differ from us in profound ways we find uncomfortable. Toxic ideas promote some extreme agenda like racism, terrorism, and fascism. Toxic ideas are those which have historically laid waste to communities and people, as the Nazi ideals did to Europe during the twentieth century or the hateful rhetoric that led to the Rwandan genocide. Regrettably, some tend to brand everything as "extreme" these days. The problem is: if you cry wolf long enough, no one will pay attention. If everything is extreme, then nothing is. Many ideas and practices considered normal forty years ago are now being condemned as "extreme." How can this be? You see, it is easy to dismiss ideas that you don't like or that seem new or that you don't understand, simply because they are strange to you. It takes discipline and hard work to be slow to judge and quick to listen. God grant us wisdom.

It takes discipline and hard work to be slow to judge and quick to listen.

On the other side, there are people and ideas worth listening to and considering. They may come from different countries, speak different languages, and have vastly different life experiences from us. If we will suspend judgment for a while and truly listen, we may gain a friend and learn something valuable.

I want to introduce you to someone who I think is worth listening to: Fethullah Gülen. He is a Turkish Muslim scholar, a prolific writer, and the source of inspiration for millions of moderately inclined Muslims around the world. Gülen was born in 1941 near Erzurum, Turkey. He grew up in a religiously observant home, the son of an imam (the person who leads prayers and religious education in a mosque). He became a state preacher in 1959 and took his first post in Izmir, a prominent city on Turkey's western coast. Inspired by the teachings of Said Nursi (1877–1960) and Mevlana Jalal ad-Din Rumi (1207–1263), Gülen advocates a spiritual form of Islam that is open to science, promotes education, and is deeply committed to tolerance and interfaith dialogue. One of his principal ideas is *hizmet*, the notion that all true believers in God have a duty to serve the common good of the community, nation, and world. As a result, he has inspired a transnational civic movement often referred to as the Gülen movement.[1] His followers have founded schools (more than five hundred) and hospitals, and have organized various charitable and educational institutions in countries around the world. In his books, publications, and audio recordings, Gülen condemns terrorism as un-Islamic and appeals instead for understanding, tolerance, and dialogue based on religious principles. In the late 1990s, Gülen immigrated to the United States for health reasons, although many critics suspect that it had more to do with tensions between him and secular Turkish authorities. A few years ago, Turkish officials accused Gülen of advocating the establishment of an Islamic state in Ataturk's secular Turkey. Given the conditions in the Middle East, this could have been a serious charge if it were true. But there was no evidence that Gülen had political interests, and he was later acquitted. Gülen's unique brand of Islam is deeply spiritual and contemplative, yet there is a social component which seeks to elevate all people regardless of their faiths. For that reason, Gülen deserves to be heard. But where do we begin? Space does not permit us to consider everything Gülen says on subjects like education in the sciences, harmonizing intellectual and spiritual development, and engaging in a caring, humane activism. So we will limit ourselves to remarks that Gülen has made regarding tolerance and interfaith dialogue, subjects close to our own interests in this book.

Although Gülen has been shaped in a different world culturally and religiously from most of us, you will be surprised to discover the amazing resonances which exist between his thinking and ours on issues like tolerance. He defines tolerance as embracing all people regardless of differences and having the ability to put up with habits and issues we personally dislike by drawing upon the strength of convictions, conscience, faith, and a generous heart.[2] Now, this stands in sharp contrast to those who advocate that tolerance means that we must set aside our convictions and faith traditions in order to make progress.

Many people involved in the tolerance and interfaith dialogue movements grew up with deep faiths and have since abandoned them. Still, they have a residue of faith that remains and often remember that religious people experience their faiths at deep, visceral levels. For some of them, faith becomes an impediment to progress. For Gülen, the vitality of faith is what motivates true believers to work toward a more peaceful world.

One of the key concepts that Gülen uses in discussions of tolerance is *hoshgoru* (*hosh* = good or pleasant; *goru* = view). Sometimes this word is translated into English as "tolerance," but conceptually it is probably best to take it as "empathetic acceptance." For Gülen, tolerance involves identifying with and accepting others regardless of the differences between you. But no one can identify with another without first listening to them and understanding the world from which they come. The adage "walk a mile in my shoes" comes to mind.

Unlike many moderns who wish to eliminate differences between groups and assimilate them into the mainstream majority, Gülen argues that embracing and celebrating our differences demonstrates respect for those traditions which otherwise will be left out. Furthermore, Gülen locates the resources necessary to create an atmosphere of tolerance and dialogue precisely in the particularity of every faith community. He believes that each faith tradition carries within it what it takes not only to bear vibrant witness to that faith but also to show generosity and hospitality to those outside it. For Gülen, the essence of Islam—like the word *islam*—involves surrender to God, peace, contentment, and security. He cites a well-known episode from the life of the prophet Muhammad. When asked what practice of the faith is most beneficial, Muhammad answered, "Feeding the hungry and offering *salaam* (the greeting of peace) to both friend and stranger."[3] Essentially, the pursuit of peace and seeking to establish peace are fundamental values to Islam, according to Gülen. If peace is better, as the Quran teaches, then true Muslims must work toward peace.

For Gülen, tolerance is ultimately rooted in the attributes of God. Allah (the Arabic word for "God") is all-forgiving, all-merciful, all-compassionate. If Allah is all these things, as all the prophets and messengers of the past have said, then the people of Allah must themselves be forgiving, merciful, and compassionate, as well. These attributes of God have been communicated most effectively through the Quran and the Sunna (oral and written traditions regarding the way Muhammad and his companions practiced the faith). So, for example, the Quran calls all Muslims to engage in dialogue and demonstrate tolerance because it is in the nature of Allah (64:14). Although a true believer may defend himself from an enemy's attack, Allah does not forbid showing kindness and acting justly to those non-Muslims who are willing to live together with Muslims in peace (60:8). True believers are called to forgive those who do not look forward to the Days of God (45:14). Likewise, they are to swallow their anger and forgive others when they have been harmed (3:134). Gülen cites these passages and many others to show that the Quran itself is "the source of leniency and tolerance." Beyond that, Gülen relates a number of episodes from the life of the Prophet and his companions to show that he was a man of peace and demonstrated peace in his relationships with friends, enemies, and "People of the Book" (referring to Jews, Christians, and perhaps Zoroastrians).

Now, Gülen does not skirt the problem cited by many: namely, the negative statements made about Jews and Christians in the Quran. According to Gülen, these injunctions are not universal directives by Allah. These negative statements reflect the doctrinal controversies and active hostilities that were going on at the time between these different communities. Clearly, the Quran criticizes certain beliefs held by Jews and Christians (such as claiming that God has a son or granting certain powers to the clergy). However, these critiques are leveled against ideas and doctrines, not people. Furthermore, those verses of the Quran that permit fighting are based on situations when there were skirmishes and battles waged against the young Muslim community by Jews, Christians, or pagan groups on the Arab peninsula. In a sense, these Quranic verses must be explained the way Hebrew and biblical scholars discuss the holy war in the Old Testament between Israel and her enemies. God's directive to Saul to wipe out the Amalekites was a one-time order;

it was not to be repeated. On the whole, Gülen holds that the Quran is balanced toward civilized, peaceful coexistence while preserving Muslim identity and practices. This was important, of course, because in the seventh century AD Muslims were a small majority seeking acceptance in a world that was reluctant to grant any recognition to a new religion.

For Gülen, there is another important reason why tolerance is so important for the true believer: the interrelatedness of all things. Gülen starts with the idea that love is the reason for creation and existence, and that everything in the world is God's handiwork. If this is so, if you do not approach all people who are creatures of God with love, then you hurt those who love God and whom God loves. Essentially, you cannot claim to love God without loving everything God has made. Love, of course, is an essential pillar of tolerance, as we propose here.

> **If we will suspend judgment for a while and truly listen, we may gain a friend and learn something valuable.**

The interrelatedness of all things leads Gülen to practice what Baptist theologian A. J. Conyers calls an "open soul." Gülen has famously written, "Be so tolerant that your heart becomes wide like the ocean. Become inspired with faith and love for others. Offer a hand to those in trouble, and be concerned about everyone."[4] For Gülen, faith in Allah and love for his creation serve as twin pillars for a kind of tolerance that makes one's heart as wide as the ocean. Practically speaking, this is worked out in deeds of generosity, compassion, and hospitality directed toward everyone, regardless of their need. Similarly, Gülen has said, "Applaud the good for their goodness, appreciate those who have believing hearts, and be kind to believers. Approach unbelievers so gently that their envy and hatred melt away."[5] Now, Gülen does not limit the word *believers* to fellow Muslims, but to People of the Book (Jews and Christians) and, by extension, to all people. He bases this on the Quranic teaching that calls Muslims to accept the earlier prophets and their books (2:2–4) and to act kindly and justly toward all non-Muslims as long as they are not actively trying to fight against you (60:8). But this kind of openness must be balanced when it comes to people who would oppress and threaten you; so Gülen warns that there must be limits to tolerance when he writes: "Being merciful to a cobra means being unjust to the people the cobra has bitten."[6]

Now, as we have suggested earlier, the practice of the "open soul" depends on humility. Humility for Gülen means judging "your worth in the Creator's sight by how much space He occupies in your heart and your worth in people's eyes by how you treat them."[7] We see in this statement evidence of the spiritual side of Islam, a kind of mysticism typical of the Sufi tradition. The human heart is made for its Creator and is at its best—namely, humble and generous—when the All-Forgiving and All-Merciful One fills every corner. Unlike many practitioners of Islam we see today in the news and read about on the Internet, Gülen privileges the spiritual sphere of Islam over the institutional and political spheres. This means that a person's commitment to the vitality of his or her spiritual life manifests itself in treating others with compassion, forgiveness, love, and tolerance. Such generous treatment of others will be noticed and appreciated, and will result in kind treatment in return.

For Gülen, the practice of tolerance—with roots firmly planted in the Quran and the Sunna (the way of the Prophet)—finds its ultimate expression in interfaith and intercultural dialogue. This is similar to what we have called developing a "listening heart." On the strength of his own teaching and example, Gülen has been able to accomplish more than any leader I know to inspire a generation of young people who are taking the message of love, tolerance, and dialogue to the nations. In particular, Gülen has urged his followers to establish organizations committed to dialogue and tolerance everywhere they live. He has recommended that tolerance awards be given to encourage leaders from various faith communities to work together toward peaceful coexistence. In order to make possible such enormous changes in the social landscape, Gülen has warned that tolerance and dialogue will be costly ventures that will take many decades (indeed lifetimes) to see the full fruit.

Interfaith dialogue, according to Gülen and his followers, will involve people committed to their respective faiths coming together and bearing witness to their faiths for the express purpose of mutual understanding, empathy, appreciation, enrichment, and cooperation. Dialogue must not have as its goal proselytizing or attempting to convert others. It is not about debating the merits and demerits of a particular faith. It is not about assessing the various truth claims of another's faith. It is definitely not an attempt to unify all faiths or create a single world religion. It is also not about compromising one's own faith or watering it down for safe consumption.[8]

Anyone who approaches dialogue with hidden agendas will find the engagement frustrating, polarizing, and ultimately a failure. Successes in interfaith dialogue will come slowly as sincere individuals come together to share the stories that have shaped their lives. A few years ago, Walter Brueggemann came to Houston Baptist University to give the prestigious A. O. Collins Lectures in Theology. While there, he made an interesting and provocative statement. He said, "The difference between Jews, Christians, and Muslims is rather simple. We tell each other different stories." He went on to say that Jews gather in their homes and synagogues and tell each other one set of stories. Christians gather in churches and cathedrals and tell each other a different set of stories. Muslims gather in mosques and do the same with yet another group of stories. In the end, many of the differences between us can be traced to the different stories we tell. Brueggemann, a narrative theologian, is convinced that stories shape our lives, individually and corporately, in profound and ultimate ways. We cannot escape their power. What Brueggemann did not say is that, though the reason for the differences may be simple, the differences themselves are not. They are profound. And though we may find common ground among all the world's religions, we must not neglect the significant ways in which our faiths differ. By learning the truth about others and their faiths, by respecting the differences that exist between all of God's creation, we will find our own faiths enriched, our commitments deepened, and perhaps we will help create a world where God's peace, God's *shalom*, can reign.

Finally, Gülen understands the crucial role that forgiveness and non-retaliation play in creating the kind of sacred space where tolerance can flourish. He refers to forgiveness as a great virtue that is paramount to tolerance. Forgiveness restores us and our world in ways that no other action can. To be forgiven is to be repaired. And yet one cannot seek forgiveness without forgiving others, for as Gülen said, "The road to forgiveness passes through the act of forgiving."[9] But like tolerance, there must be limits to forgiveness. To forgive people who engage in monstrous evil and delight in the suffering of others is to disrespect forgiveness itself. Furthermore, we have no right to forgive such people, for to forgive them is to disrespect the people who have suffered so much from their hands. Similarly, a person committed to tolerance must also be committed to non-retaliation. According to Gülen, tolerance will manifest itself in halting verbal attacks or refusing

> **By learning the truth about others and their faiths . . . we will find our own faiths enriched.**

to abuse unbelievers; true Muslims must swallow their anger and forgive as the Quran has directed (3:134). Citing the Turkish poet and Sufi mystic Yunus Emre (1240?–1321?), Gülen encourages those who have been attacked to act as if they have no hand or tongue with which to strike back.[10]

Clearly, for Gülen, forgiveness and a commitment to non-retaliation are foundational to authentic tolerance. The reason seems obvious. For most of his life, Gülen has labored in a part of the world where injustice and suffering are the ambient reality, where retaliation is normal, and where forgiveness is a distant stranger. Unfortunately, Gülen's teaching on peace, tolerance, and dialogue is not followed by all Muslims. His voice is often muted—if not silenced—by political elements within certain branches of Islam that tend toward restricting freedoms and imposing more extreme versions of Islam on one another. Despite this, the Gülen movement represents a hopeful trend among moderate Muslims which we hope and pray will convince Muslims everywhere of its truth and value.

In my view, Gülen is worth knowing and listening to, whether you are Muslim, Christian, Jew, or agnostic. Many in the West and America have an impression of Islam based primarily on news reports of violence around the world. You may be one of them. But before you judge too quickly and conclude that "all Muslims are violent," it would be best to listen to moderate Muslims like Gülen. They offer a competing narrative which has nothing to do with violent jihad but everything to do with faithfulness to God and service to others.

In earlier chapters, we talked about how earlier generations of Christians studied the pagan poets, quoted from Greek literature, drew from non-Christian philosophers, and adopted various practices from other religions. They did so because they were convinced that truth, beauty, and goodness were real and had to be real for everyone. Accordingly, they thought God had revealed Himself partially in those cultures and, by studying them, they could deepen and widen their Christian faith. Similarly, C. S. Lewis studied the Norse and Greek myths of dying and rising gods, only to discover that, in the resurrection of Jesus of Nazareth, "myth" had become "fact." All of these Christian thinkers and influencers had something in common; they believed that the final, full, and definitive revelation about God had come through Jesus the Liberating King. While the literature and culture of other religions did not contain the complete revelation, they did express (imperfectly) aspects of the truth. By studying and listening to these other cultures, they did not think they were hampering their faith; indeed, they found that they were enhancing it. Here is why: they did not begin with the assumption that all Greeks, Romans, Egyptians, and pagans were wrong about everything. In other words, they were slow to judge and quick to listen. Now, it is important to note that they did not accept everything from these other religions. That would have been foolish and contradictory. After studying them carefully, they rejected much of what these other religions taught. But they continued to press forward, confident in the fact that the God who had been at work through Jesus had also been at work through creation and in human history. This is what theologians refer to as natural or general revelation.

All of these Christian thinkers ... believed that the final, full, and definitive revelation about God has come through Jesus the Liberating King.

We will do well to have the same mind and attitude as these earlier generations of saints. Like them, we must be slow to judge and quick to listen. This does not mean that we should accept everything we hear. Nor does it mean that we should just assume that everyone other than us (Christians) is wrong about everything. What I am suggesting is that we are able to listen to the best Muslim, Jewish, Buddhist, Hindu, and even atheist writers looking for common ground, expecting to find something of value. If we will suspend judgment and listen to leaders like Fethullah Gülen with no other agenda, we will discover that our own faith has broadened and deepened.

Before we conclude this chapter, I want to leave you with a few thoughts about interfaith dialogue. Too often, interfaith dialogue events take place, but the right people are not at the table. I know. I have been to many of these meetings and even hosted a few. Too often, interfaith dialogue is just a matter of "preaching to the choir." The people who attend are curious about religion but not committed to a religion. The people who participate have a residue of religion but no longer its robustness. The people who plan interfaith gatherings are often people who think that all religions are pretty much the same; so, they think, no one should get bent out of shape over the discussion because it's not a big deal anyway. Instead, I argue that we need the kind of people at the table who say: "This I believe. I can do no other. Here I stand." Until these kinds of people come to the table—whether they be Christian, Muslim, Hindu, or Jew—I'm afraid that most efforts at interfaith dialogue will not be effective. True interfaith dialogue is not a celebration of sameness. The most authentic moments of dialogue take place in discomfort and tension. They are spoken with an edge in the voice. They are stated when you move forward slightly in your chair. They are heard when someone sinks into their seat and folds their arms defiantly. These are moments of authentic dialogue. They can proceed and will proceed only as long as they are rooted in real relationships between people of different faiths.

With the church, let us pray: "Father, give us the wisdom we need to see and appreciate truth wherever it may be found."

))) QUESTIONS TO CONSIDER:

1. Did you find any points of agreement with Fethullah Gülen? If so, what are they?

2. Do you have friends from other faiths? How have their friendships influenced you?

3. Christians are often afraid to engage in any kind of interfaith dialogue because they fear it will weaken their commitments. How can you keep that from happening?

4. What kind of people do you think ought to be involved in interfaith dialogue?

5. You have thoughts and opinions about Islam, Buddhism, Hinduism, and other religions. What sources have shaped your thinking? How reliable are they? Where could you find even better resources?

LISTENING TO THE PAGANS:
C. S. LEWIS

If you are a Christian you do not have to believe that all the other religions are simply wrong all through.

—C. S. Lewis[1]

C. S. Lewis strikes me as a person who exemplified the kinds of attitudes and actions we have been talking about in this book. He bore witness to his faith and defended it against detractors, and he did so effectively without being considered judgmental. He was slow to judge and quick to listen. In this chapter, I want to explore some of what C. S. Lewis wrote, in the hopes that we can learn from his example.

C. S. Lewis was probably the foremost apologist and Christian thinker in the twentieth century. He was born Clive Staples Lewis in Belfast, Ireland on November 29, 1898. After enlisting in the British army and surviving trench warfare in World War I, he returned to Oxford and completed his studies. During his career, he held academic posts at two of the world's great universities, Oxford and Cambridge. "Jack," as his friends called him, is probably best known for his fictional works, such as *The Narnia Chronicles*, *The Space Trilogy*, and *The Screwtape Letters*. But he was also a deep thinker and apologist for the Christian faith, as is evident in a number of well-known books and essays which have gone on to be classics: *Mere Christianity, Miracles,* and *The Problem of Pain,* to name a few. Lewis's imaginative approach in his writings and his generous use of symbols and analogies to express deep truths has left an indelible mark on the lives of millions of Christians.[2]

Lewis had a lifelong fascination with myths from other cultures, particularly myths associated with dying and rising gods. These stories were as diverse as the cultures that spawned them, which explains in part why scholars find them so controversial. Yet they are present in most of the ancient cultures known to the West: Norse, Canaanite, Egyptian, Roman, and Greek. Some of the names of the gods are familiar to those who have studied mythology or read the Bible: Balder, Baal, Adonis, Tammuz, Osiris, Dionysius, Persephone. While

> **Since God is light and in Him there is no darkness, any light visible in other religions—no matter how faint or flickering—must be attributed to Him.**

each story is unique, there are some commonalities. In many of the stories, a central character dies, goes down to the underworld, and then in some sense comes back to life. When they are "resurrected," they achieve some benefit back on earth, such as fertility for next year's crops or the coming of warmth and light in the spring. These myths are often associated with agricultural rituals. This makes sense, given how dependent the ancients were on the success of their crops year by year. The dying and rising of the Egyptian god Osiris, for example, parallels the receding and rising of the waters of the Nile so critical for life to flourish along the path of the river. The god who dies and comes back doesn't always come back personally and literally; in some cases, the "rising" is more figurative.

Lewis left his Christian upbringing during his adolescent years due in large part to the fact that his schoolmasters had told him that Christianity was 100 percent correct, while all the other religions—including the pagan myths he loved—were 100 percent wrong. The young Lewis rejected this narrow view of other faiths and ultimately walked away from the church.

When Lewis came back to the faith at age thirty-two and joined the Anglican Communion, it was largely because of the influence of other academics, such as his friend J. R. R. Tolkien. Lewis came to regard Christianity as the "true myth," compared to "men's myths" in paganism. But rather than seeing the difference between them as black and white, for Lewis it represented various shades of grey.

The fact that there were similarities between pagan myths and the true myth did not lead Lewis to conclude "so much the worse for Christianity." Rather, it led him to conclude "so much the better for paganism." As British scholar and Lewis expert Michael Ward writes, "Paganism contained a good deal of meaning that was realized, consummated and perfected in Christ."[3] For Lewis, pagan myths amounted to a prefiguration of Christ. If the Christian faith is the highest expression of God's revelation to man, as Lewis believed, then there must have been lower expressions on the way—not just in Judaism, but in all or most of the other cultures around the world. In other words, these earlier or natural revelations were like lower rungs of a ladder that led inevitably to the heights achieved in Christianity.

In his famous essay "Myth Became Fact," Lewis wrote, "We must not be nervous about 'parallels' and 'Pagan Christs': they ought to be there—it would be a stumbling block if they weren't."[4] Likewise, the similarities between the Norse or Roman gods and the one true God of the Bible "ought to be there." It would be odd if they were not. Since God is light and in Him there is no darkness, any light visible in other religions—no matter how faint or flickering—must be attributed to Him. Lewis refused to judge these pagan myths as deficient—as his schoolmasters had done—and instead tried to listen to what they were saying about those who taught them and heard them. These myths had codified the wisdom and insight of vast cultures which existed for centuries. Did they indeed have nothing worth saying? Lewis didn't think so. Although their wisdom is not as complete as that found in Christ, rather than despising them and condemning them for not being the fullness, these cultures and their stories ought to be admired.

Lewis found in the literature of the ancient and medieval worlds—and modern world for that matter—a longing for transcendence, meaning, beauty, and truth. This is Humanity 101. That longing finds its ultimate satisfaction in the incarnation, life, death, and resurrection of Jesus of Nazareth. While some people look down on paganism and judge it to be false, negative, and a human-constructed path to the gods, Lewis saw in these stories a shadow of the gospel. How could he do that? Because he was slow to judge and quick to listen.

We can find a similar approach and a willingness to listen to others in the story of Paul and the Athenians. The Athenians were inquisitive people. They loved to spend their time talking and debating various ideas. So when Paul came to their city, they invited him to speak at the Areopagus, a venue where intellectuals and the curious gathered occasionally for discussions and debates. Paul accepted their invitation and addressed them in Acts 17:22–28:

> **PAUL:** [22] Athenians, *as I have walked your streets*, I have observed your strong and diverse religious ethos. You truly are a religious people. [23] I have stopped again and again to examine carefully the religious statues and inscriptions that fill your city. On one such altar, I read this inscription: "TO

AN UNKNOWN GOD." I am not here to tell you about a
strange foreign deity, but about this One whom you already
worship, though without full knowledge. [24] This is the God
who made the universe and all it contains, the God who is the
King of all heaven and all earth. It would be illogical to assume
that a God of this magnitude could possibly be contained
in any man-made structure, no matter how majestic. [25] Nor
would it be logical to think that this God would need human
beings to provide Him with food and shelter—after all, He
Himself would have given to humans everything they need—
life, breath, *food, shelter, and so on.*

[26] This God made us in all our diversity from one original
person, allowing each culture to have its own time to develop,
giving each its own place to live and thrive in its distinct
ways. [27] *His purpose in all this was* that people *of every culture
and religion* would search for this ultimate God, grope for
Him *in the darkness, as it were,* hoping to find Him. Yet, in
truth, God is not far from any of us. [28] For *you know the saying,*
"We live in God; we move in God; we exist in God." And still
another said, "We are indeed God's children."

Rather than criticize and berate the Athenians for being completely wrong about their gods and religions, Paul sought to find
common ground. The common ground approach was integral to
his mission strategy. He spent time with them. He watched them,
observed them, read their inscriptions, and ultimately commended
them for being a very religious people. In every way possible, he gave
them the benefit of the doubt. As he walked through the streets of
the city, he found that they already had an altar to an unknown god.
Paul took this as an opening to introduce them to the Creator God,
the Father of our Lord Jesus Christ.

Notice what Paul did next. He began quoting the Athenians' own poets. He did not quote them long chapters of the Hebrew prophets and poets. He did not rehearse for them the Jewish law. Instead, he had taken time to listen to and memorize some of their poets and prophets. How many of us have taken time to read the poets and prophets of Islam, Hinduism, and Buddhism? How many of us could quote their sages? Well, Paul could, because he was slow to judge and quick to listen.

Quoting Epimenedes, a sixth century BC Greek poet, Paul says, "We live in God; we move in God; we exist in God." Now, when Epimenedes recited his verse, he was referring to Zeus as the god in whom they lived, moved, and had their being. Paul redirects them to another possibility: this might refer to the unknown Creator God rather than Zeus. In other words, Paul says, "You're right to say that in God we live, move, and exist, but that god is not the one you are thinking of; it is none other than the one you worship as 'unknown.'" This was the God Epimenedes was talking about, even if he didn't know it.

> **Paul did not make his point by belittling the Athenians and saying, "You are completely wrong."**

Second, Paul quoted Aratus, a Greek poet who flourished about 300 BC. The apostle said, "And still another [of your poets] said, 'We are indeed God's children.'" Now again, Aratus was referring to Zeus, and Paul leverages that remark to refer them to the one true God. In effect, Paul is respectfully submitting that what the Greek poets had said of Zeus finds its ultimate expression in the one true God who was the Father of the Lord Jesus Christ.

Paul did not make his point by belittling the Athenians and saying, "You are completely wrong." No, his approach was, "Hey, you're on to something here. Let me tell you what I think it is." As Michael Ward has written:

> . . . it only makes sense to meet people where they are. Where else, indeed, can they be met? Before people know the God and Father of the Lord Jesus Christ, they are not in a state of complete innocence or ignorance about the divine nature. Everyone after a certain age has thoughts and beliefs about what is of ultimate value in the universe, that is what is "divine." Those thoughts need to be recognized and responded to. Sometimes the response will consist in a contradiction, but more often than not there will be something that can be responded to positively, that can be coaxed into a fuller life and brighter light. This is why Lewis can say, "the only possible basis for Christian apologetics is a proper respect for paganism." Paganism must be "looked back at"—re-spected—in order for the Christian apologist to see whether or how much it needs opposition.[5]

Paul's common ground approach made him immediately successful in many of the cities he visited. The apostle traveled to dozens of cities in Asia Minor and Greece and left behind congregations in each city. Luke tells us that he left the Areopagus that day having made several new converts (Acts 17:32–34) even if some of the elite scoffed at him. Paul's exchange with the Athenians is one of the most potent examples I know of cross-cultural evangelism in the Bible. He starts with common ground, provokes his audience to think, and then invites them to pursue God in new ways. He doesn't condemn them for their wrong beliefs, nor does he attempt to water down the gospel. He doesn't offer them easy acronyms; instead, he connects their culture with the truth and beauty of the gospel revealed in Jesus the Liberating King.

Theologians refer to this common core of beliefs held by all people—Buddhists, Christians, Muslims, Jews, etc.—as natural or general revelation. To all humans is given or unveiled something of the divine, the true, the good, the beautiful. As the Scriptures say, the rain falls on the just and the unjust (Matt. 5:45 NKJV). This general revelation comes to all humanity mediated through creation, human reason, a basic universal morality, and human experience. It was codified in our nation's Declaration of Independence, "We hold these truths to be self-evident, that all men are created equal, that they are endowed by their Creator with certain unalienable Rights, that among these are Life, Liberty and the pursuit of Happiness." Self-evident truths are assumptions which need no argument. They are our starting place. Why? Because everyone can see that they are true. That is what "self-evident" means. These truths are found in general revelation. The equality of all men and the fact that rights are given by God, not kings, may be consistent with what you find in Christian Scripture and tradition, but our founders did not discover them in the pages of Scripture. They examined history, used reason, and pondered creation to discover these self-evident truths. Paul refers to this reality in his letter to the Roman Christians (Rom. 1:19–21):

> [19] These people [those who intentionally do wrong] are not ignorant about what can be known of God, because He has shown it to them *with great clarity*. [20] From the beginning, creation in its magnificence enlightens us to His nature. Creation itself makes His undying power and divine identity clear, even though they are invisible; and it voids the excuses *and ignorant claims* of these people [21] because, despite the fact that they knew the one true God, they have failed to show the *love*, honor, and appreciation due to the One who created them! Instead, their lives are consumed by vain thoughts that poison their foolish hearts.

Paul was well-versed in the Jewish Scriptures. He could have quoted them to make his case, but he didn't need to, nor did he mean to. An appeal to what creation reveals about God was sufficient to make his point and reorient them toward a better way of living.

Both Paul and C. S. Lewis would agree that the Light of the World has enlightened all, not just those who are already Christians. Because all people are made in the image and likeness of God, they have access to reason, virtue, and an imagination already inspired by the breath of life. The spiritual impulse possessed by all people reflects the goodness and wisdom of the one true Creator God. So it must be respected (looked back at) regardless of where it is found. Still, Christian theology has never held that this general or natural revelation is sufficient to bring about the salvation of the soul, much less the world. More was needed through God's self-revelation in Jesus, the Liberating King, and in time the holy Scriptures. Roger Olson observes, "*That* God is revealed in nature—including creation itself, human conscience and possibly history as a whole (universal history)—has seldom been denied [by theologians] and almost always assumed. But *the benefit* of that general revelation of God has always been questioned."[6] Few Christian theologians deny the existence and reality of general revelation; none, as far as I know, deny the necessity of the more specific revelation that comes through Scripture and the incarnation.

In *Mere Christianity*, Lewis writes:

> If you are a Christian you do not have to believe that all the other religions are simply wrong all through. If you are an atheist you do have to believe that the main point in all the religions of the whole world is simply one huge mistake. If you are a Christian, you are free to think that all those religions, even the queerest ones, contain at least some hint of the truth. When I was an atheist I had to try and persuade myself that most of the human race have always been wrong about the question that mattered

to them most; when I became a Christian I was able to take a more liberal view.[7]

Now, Lewis was writing many years ago when words like *queer* and *liberal* were not loaded terms. We must be careful not to miss his meaning simply because we live in a different age. The word *queer* in this statement means "odd" and has nothing to do with sexuality. He is suggesting that a bit of the truth can be found in all religions, even in the ones which seem most odd to us. But you cannot know that bit of truth if you've already decided that all religions except yours are flat wrong. You must not prejudge them before you study them; and it is best not to judge them as you study them. Rather, you must be willing to listen to what they say regard-

> [C.S. Lewis] was quick to listen and slow to judge, which makes him an excellent example for us to follow.

ing the most crucial questions of life. Likewise, the word *liberal* here means "generous" and has nothing to do with any political ideology. According to Lewis, after he became a Christian, he could be much more generous to the majority of people in the world who followed some form of faith. Lewis confessed that, when he was an atheist, he was not generous—he could not be—because he was convinced that most of the world was following a big lie. It was the Christian Lewis, not the atheist Lewis, who was the least judgmental and most generous when it came to his fellow man.

C. S. Lewis was a person who stood up for his faith, answered his critics effectively, and did so from a generous orthodoxy. I dare say we'd have to look long and hard to find the slightest hint of a judgmental tone in his writings. He was quick to listen and slow to judge, which makes him an excellent example for us to follow.

With Paul let us pray that the Father will grant us the light to see His true nature in all of creation.

QUESTIONS TO CONSIDER:

1. How is it possible to be orthodox in faith and yet generous as we approach people of other faiths or people with no faith at all?

2. Paul bore effective witness to Christ because he knew the pagan poets and philosophers. What should we know today in order to be effective witnesses?

3. What can we take away from the writings of C. S. Lewis to help us be quick to listen and slow to judge?

CONCLUSION

Many years ago, I had a professor who began the term with these words, "The most important word in the English language is *relationship*." It was a mantra he repeated often that semester. The more I have thought about him and his course, the more confident I am that he is correct. But the problem is that relationships—regardless of the type (family, friend, coworker)—take time to develop and time to mature. We can't rush into relationships. If we do, the results can be either silly or disastrous. Still, culture is moving at such a quick pace that it is hard to slow down, listen, and take time to get to know another person. Many of the solutions to the problems we face in our modern culture are found precisely in this word *relationship*. Are we willing to deal with people who are different only at arm's length, or are we willing to enter into true friendship with them? Are we content to stand back and prejudge others while being pre-judged by them, or are we ready to sit down over coffee or a meal and begin to share our unique stories?

Slow to Judge opened with the realization that Christians are not only perceived as but actually can be judgmental in their approach to other people. Judgment, of course, is not always wrong, but it's always wrong to pre-judge or judge too quickly. Exercising judgment is necessary if we wish to create a just and good society, but it is the attitude of judgment fueled by pride that causes us so much grief. It is possible to stand up for your faith, defend it against detractors, and do so without a judgmental, I'm-better-than-you attitude. What it takes is a commitment to be slow to judge and quick to listen. What it takes is a willingness to have real relationships with people different from you. That can be unsettling and risky, but it can also be worth the risk.

Along the way, we've explored various themes from Scripture:

- the wisdom of a listening heart
- the necessity of correction in the church
- the danger of judging by appearances
- the consequences of showing respect
- the primacy and character of love
- the benefits of forgiveness
- the damage done by the words and labels we use
- the peril of pride
- the exalted place of humility
- the blessing of hospitality and practicing an open soul
- the need for authentic tolerance
- the purpose of the church's mission

In the final chapters of the book, we turned our attention to two outstanding people, each for different reasons. My hope in both cases is that all of us can learn something valuable by suspending judgment and truly listening to them.

In 2013, *Time* magazine named Fethullah Gülen, Turkish educator and Islamic scholar, to its list of the one hundred most influential people in the world. As the Muslim faith continues to grow globally—particularly in the West—and as the threat from extremist elements in Islam build, we would do well to get to know and listen to those moderate Muslim voices. These leaders may well hold the key to stemming the tide of radical factions in their own religion. We can work with people like Gülen and his millions of followers to counter the more militant, strident voices clamoring to be heard.

A few years ago, I presented a paper to a conference being held at the University of London. After my presentation, I stopped in to listen to a British security expert discuss the threat of global terrorism. His opening line was, "In the future, we will fight terrorism with technology," but his PowerPoint didn't work. I thought to myself, "Boy, are we in trouble? We're going to fight terrorism with technology and we can't even get PowerPoint to work!" No doubt, technology will be important as we defend ourselves against global terror, but perhaps even more significant will be those Muslims, like Gülen, who condemn terror and can rally millions of like-minded Muslims to a kinder, gentler form of Islam. Gülen offers us an example of someone who is slow to judge and quick to listen from the Muslim religion.

Then we turned to C. S. Lewis, Christian apologist, British scholar, and prolific author. *Christianity Today* named Lewis's *Mere Christianity* the best book of the twentieth century. Lewis offers us an example of someone from inside the Christian faith who took the kind of approach we've advocated here. Lewis did not read only Christian authors and people he agreed with. He found immense pleasure and profit in studying Norse, Greek, and Irish mythology. He found meaning and longing in these stories which he believed are eventually fulfilled and satisfied in the incarnation, life, death, burial, and resurrection of Jesus. Still, residing in these "pagan" writers is an inkling of the truth revealed finally and fully in Jesus of Nazareth. Having climbed the first rung of the ladder, he was ready to make it all the way to the top.

Furthermore, Lewis looked around the world and found that all people from all faiths and no faiths at all have a standard or universal morality. He writes:

These then are the two points that I wanted to make. First, that human beings, all over the earth, have this curious idea that they ought to behave in a certain way, and cannot really get rid of it. Secondly, that they do not in fact behave in that way. They know the Law of Nature; they break it. These two facts are the foundation of all clear thinking about ourselves and the universe we live in.[1]

For Lewis to have arrived here, he had to deny himself his first impressions of these other religions. He had to study them to understand the heart of what they taught. He found in their teachings ideas similar to what we see unveiled fully in the Christian Scriptures. Lewis, perhaps better than any other twentieth century apologist, knew how important it was to suspend judgment and listen intently to outsiders.

Not long after Father Mario joined us on the radio, we had a call one night from a frustrated woman. She had discovered a year or so earlier that her only child was gay. From the conversation that evening, it seemed to all that she was still processing what that meant, even though she said she had come to grips with it. Part of her processing was to give people of faith wherever she could a hard time for not fully accepting homosexual acts as normal, natural, and beautiful aspects of human love. Her call had been prompted by some event in the news. I don't recall exactly which one, but what I do recall is Mario's thoughtful response to her.

The woman was clearly agitated and said, "Why can't you religious people accept that two men can love each other?" Mario spoke in soothing tones, calming her with a story of something he had witnessed recently. He told about two men he had met who had been in a long-term relationship. One day, the younger man tested positive for the HIV virus. It didn't take long for the virus to initiate an attack on the victim's body. In less than a year, he experienced the full onslaught of the AIDS syndrome. It came on him with fury and relentlessly assaulted system after system. His health deteriorated rapidly, and soon he was no longer able to take care of himself. Throughout the ordeal, his partner of these many years did not abandon him; he stayed right beside him. He waited on him, served him as best he could as the disease took more and more of his friend away. He cared for him in their home as long as it was possible. Eventually, the day came when both men decided it was time for hospice care. The end was coming and both men knew it. Mario testified beautifully to the love the men had for one another. While the good Father gently laid out the Catholic position—that homosexual acts are contrary to natural law and not approved by the church—he also said he had seldom seen such love and devotion between two people. He went on to extol the goodness and beauty of love wherever, whenever it is found. Quoting the old Latin hymn, he said: *ubi caritas et amor, Deus ibi est* ("where charity and love are, God is there"). Eventually, the AIDS victim died, leaving a huge, gaping hole in the heart of his partner.

I wish I could remember Father Mario's exact words that evening. Both the rabbi and I were deeply moved by the story and the way he told it. My summary of it here for you is so pale and bland compared to the honesty and brilliance of his words that evening. Unfortunately, no recording of the conversation remains. The woman caller seemed satisfied with his response. She hung up a few minutes later grateful that someone took her seriously. While Father Mario never affirmed same-sex relationships, he clearly demonstrated respect for the memory of the men by paying tribute to the depth and sincerity of the love they shared. "Where there is love, there is God."

Father Mario's response reminded me of the way C. S. Lewis approached non-Christian literature, especially the myths. Lewis was able to look carefully at the Norse and Roman stories about their gods and find in them a prefiguration of Christ. Mario had a similar approach to the complex question of human sexuality. Though the caller asked why religious folk don't accept that two men can love each other sexually—the clear implication of her question—Mario was able to affirm nonsexual aspects of that love demonstrated clearly in the humble service and loving care the well man offered his terminally ill friend. Mario was slow to judge and quick to listen; therefore, he was able to stand up for his faith that evening without being judgmental. These are the kinds of conversations which I hope will characterize us in the future: standing firm in our beliefs and values while at the same time suspending judgment and doing whatever it takes to listen for the truth, goodness, and beauty already resident in people who are so different from us. It is there if we will just recognize it.

NOTES

INTRODUCTION

1. "Curse of the Romani,"Assasin's Creed Wiki, accessed December 4, 2014, http://assassinscreed.wikia.com/wiki/Curse_of_the_Romani.

2. David Kinnaman and Gabe Lyons, *unChristian: What a New Generation Really Thinks about Christianity . . . and Why It Matters* (Grand Rapids: Baker, 2007), 28.

3. Ibid.

4. Ibid.

5. Ibid.

6. Cornelius Plantinga, *Not the Way It's Supposed to Be: A Breviary of Sin* (Grand Rapids: Eerdmans, 1995), 81, quoted from Jack Wisdom, *Get Low: Reflections on Pride and Humility* (Houston: Whitecaps Media, 2013), 8.

7. C. S. Lewis, *Mere Christianity* (New York: HarperOne, 2000), 121–2.

8. Christian Smith and Melinda Lundquist Denton, *Soul Searching: The Religious and Spiritual Lives of American Teenagers* (Oxford: Oxford University Press, 2005), 162–71.

9. Kenda Creasy Dean, *Almost Christian: What the Faith of Our Teenagers Is Telling the American Church* (Oxford: Oxford University Press, 2010), 11–12.

10. The Voice™ Bible (Nashville: Thomas Nelson, 2012), 1203.

11. Kinnaman and Lyons, *unChristian*, 186.

12. Kinnaman and Lyons, *unChristian*, 194–5.

CHAPTER 1

1. Mark McMinn, "5 Ingredients for Becoming Wise, Backed by Psychology," *The Table—The Blog of the Biola University School for Christian Thought* (blog), June 30, 2014, accessed July 14, 2014, http://www.cct.biola.edu/blog/2014/jun/30/5-Ingredients-Becoming-Wise/.

CHAPTER 2

1. Dietrich Bonhoeffer, *Life Together* (New York: Harper & Row Publishers, 1954), 110–118.

2. William H. Willimon, *What's Right with the Church: A Spirited Statement for Those Who Have Not Given Up on the Church and for Those Who Have* (San Francisco: Harper & Row Publishers, 1985), 65.

CHAPTER 3

1. Naval Admiral William H. McRaven, "University of Texas at Austin 2014 Commencement Address"; accessed June 14, 2014, www.youtube.com /watch?v=yaQZFhrW0fU.

2. Martin Luther King, "I Have a Dream Speech," August 28, 1963, accessed March 27, 2014, www.youtube.com/watch?v=smEqnnklfYs.

3. Anne Blythe, "City of Durham settles long-running lawsuit with former Duke lacrosse players," *Charlotte Observer*, May 16, 2014, accessed May 30, 2014, http://www.charlotteobserver.com/2014/05/16/4915524/city-of-durham-settles -long-running.html#.VBGw3Ce9KSM.

4. The Voice™ Bible (Nashville: Thomas Nelson, 2012), 1498.

CHAPTER 4

1. C. S. Lewis, *Mere Christianity* (New York: HarperOne, 2000), 115.

2. C. S. Lewis, *Mere Christianity: a revised and amplified edition, with a new introduction, of the three books* Broadcast Talks, Christian Behaviour and Beyond Personality (New York: HarperOne, 2000), 131–2.

3. The Voice™ Bible (Thomas Nelson, 2012), 1408.

4. Craig Keener, *Miracles: The Credibility of the New Testament Accounts* (Grand Rapids: Baker Academic, 2011).

5. Lewis, *Mere Christianity*, 115.

6. "Pope John Paul II: I Want You To Know About Forgiveness" Story & Experience, Experienceproject.com, accessed July 31, 2013, http://www .experienceproject.com/stories/Want-You-To-Know-About-Forgiveness /1258886.

7. Joseph Shapiro, "Amish Forgive School Shooter, Struggle with Grief," NPR.org, accessed June 12, 2014, http://www.npr.org/templates/story/story.php?storyId =14900930.

8. Harold Kushner, *How Good Do We Have to Be?* (Boston: Little, Brown and Company, 1996).

9. Harold Kushner, *When Bad Things Happen to Good People* (New York: Random House, 1978).

10. Jud Wilhite, "Grace City," in *unChristian: What a New Generation Really Thinks about Christianity* by David Kinnaman and Gabe Lyons (Grand Rapids: Baker, 2007), 198. See also C. S. Lewis, *Mere Christianity*, 116–17.

CHAPTER 5

1. Michael Paulson, "Fred Phelps, Anti-Gay Preacher Who Targeted Military Funerals, Dies at 84," *New York Times.com,* accessed December 4, 2014, http://www.nytimes.com/2014/03/21/us/fred-phelps-founder-of-westboro-baptist-church-dies-at-84.html?_r=0.

2. See the frequently asked questions about the Southern Baptist Convention, accessed September 9, 2014, *http://www.sbc.net/faqs.asp*; also "Baptists Denounce Latest Westboro Stunt," February 19, 2009, *ChristianityToday.com,* accessed September 9, 2014, http://www.christiantoday.com.au/article/baptists.denounce.latest.westboro.stunt/5495.htm.

3. Southern Poverty Law Center, Extremist Files, "Westboro Baptist Church," accessed December 4, 2014, http://www.splcenter.org/get-informed/intelligence-files/groups/westboro-baptist-church.

4. Anti-Defamation League, Extremism in America, "Westboro Baptist Church," accessed December 4, 2014, http://archive.adl.org/learn/ext_us/wbc/.

5. Niraj Warikoo, "Fla. pastor Terry Jones: Islam's goal is 'world domination,'"*USAToday.com,* accessed December 4, 2014, http://usatoday30.usatoday.com/news/religion/story/2012-04-07/quran-burning-pastor-mosque-protest/54103832/1.

6. David Jackson, "Obama condemns Quran burning, violence in Afghanistan," *USAToday,* April 3, 2011, accessed May 14, 2014, http://content.usatoday.com/communities/theoval/post/2011/04/obama-condemns-quran-burning-violence-in-afghanistan/1#.VKbmG9LF-So.

7. MacMillan Dictionary.com, accessed May 2, 2014, http://www.macmillandictionary.com/us/open-dictionary/entries/Christophobia.htm.

8. George Weigel, *The Cube and the Cathedral: Europe, America, and Politics without God* (New York: Basic Books, 2008), 26-27.

9. Typically, English words are derived from either a Greek or Latin root. In the case of *homodissentic,* I have combined a Greek root (*homo*) with a Latin suffix (*dissentio*). But the Greek root "homo" has become a standard part of the English language now, like "Christ" and "Islam," so it effectively operates as an English word.

CHAPTER 6

1. See A. J. Conyers' excellent book *The Long Truce: How Toleration Made the World Safe for Profit and Power* (Dallas: Spence, 2001).

2. Conor Friedersdorf, "Mozilla's Gay-Marriage Litmus Test Violates Liberal Values," April 4, 2014, *The Atlantic,* accessed May 14, 2014, http://www.theatlantic.com/politics/archive/2014/04/mozillas-gay-marriage-litmus-test-violates-liberal-values/360156/.

3. Andrew Sullivan, "The Hounding of a Heretic," April 3, 2014, accessed May 14, 2014, http://dish.andrewsullivan.com/2014/04/03/the-hounding-of-brendan-eich/.

4. Ibid.

5. John Locke, *A Letter Concerning Toleration* (Buffalo, NY: Prometheus Books, 1990), 18–19.

6. A. J. Conyers, *The Listening Heart: Vocation and the Crisis of Modern Culture* (Waco, TX: Baylor University Press, 2009), 129.

7. Conyers, *The Long Truce*, 7–8.

8. Conyers, *The Long Truce*, 6.

9. Michael Walzer, *On Toleration* (New Haven, CT: Yale University Press, 1997), 25.

10. See the essay by H. Marcuse, "Repressive Tolerance," in *A Critique of Pure Tolerance*, ed. R. P. Wolff, B. Moore, and H. Marcuse (Boston: Beacon, 1969), 95–137.

11. Drew Magary, "What the Duck?" *GQ* (January 2014), accessed March 1, 2014, http://www.gq.com/entertainment/television/201401/duck-dynasty-phil-robertson.

12. Patrick Kevin Day, "A&E puts 'Duck Dynasty' star on hiatus following anti-gay comments," *Los Angeles Times*, December 18, 2013, accessed March 16, 2014, http://articles.latimes.com/2013/dec/18/entertainment/la-et-st-ae-puts-duck-dynasty-star-on-hiatus-following-antigay-comments-20131218.

13. Jerry Walls, "Duck Dynasty and the Scourge of Fundamentalist Intolerance" on *School of Christian Thought: Houston Baptist University* (blog), December 19, 2013, accessed January 31, 2014, http://christianthought.hbu.edu/2013/12/20/duck-dynasty-bestiality-and-ultimate-reality/.

CHAPTER 7

1. *Merriam-Webster* online dictionary, accessed February 28, 2014, http://www.merriam-webster.com/dictionary/tolerance.

2. A.J. Conyers, *The Long Truce* (Dallas: Spence, 2001), 231–32.

3. Thomas Hobbes, *Leviathan: Or the Matter, Forme, and Power of a Common-Wealth Ecclesiasticall and Civill* (Cambridge: University Press, 1904), 84.

4. Thomas Helwys, *The Mistery of Iniquity* (originally published 1612; reprint, London: Kingsgate, 1935), 69.

5. I'm grateful to my friend Dr. Larry Hurtado, University of Edinburgh, for this particular phrase.

6. Conyers, *The Long Truce*, 33.

7. Conyers, *The Long Truce*, 244.

8. Amy G. Oden, *And You Welcomed Me: A Sourcebook on Hospitality in Early Christianity* (Nashville: Abingdon, 2000), 14.

9. A. J. Conyers, *The Listening Heart: Vocation and the Crisis of Modern Culture* (Waco, TX: Baylor University Press, 2009), 136.

10. To learn more about how Paul wrote his letters, see E. R. Richards, *Paul and First-Century Letter Writing: Secretaries, Composition and Collection* (Downers Grove, IL: InterVarsity Academic, 2004).

11. The term *codex* (plural *codices*) refers primarily to hand-written manuscripts made up of papyrus and vellum pages which have been folded, stacked, and bound along one edge. Modern books are made in codex form, but are not called codices because they are produced by machines, not by hand. See Larry Hurtado, *The Earliest Christian Artifacts: Manuscripts and Christian Origins* (Grand Rapids: Eerdmans, 2006).

12. David B. Capes, "*Imitatio Christi* and the Early Worship of Jesus," in *The Jewish Roots of Christological Monotheism: Papers from the St. Andrews Conference on the Historical Origins of the Worship of Jesus*, ed. Carey C. Newman, James R. Davila, and Gladys S. Lewis (Leiden: E. J. Brill; JSJsupp, 1999), 293–307.

13. For more, see Robin M. Jensen, *Understanding Early Christian Art* (New York: Routledge, 2000).

CHAPTER 8

1. For a useful description of the Gülen movement written by an insider who also happens to be a social scientist, see Muhammed Çetin, *The Gülen Movement: Civic Service without Borders* (New York: Blue Dome Press, 2009).

2. Fethullah Gülen, *Toward a Global Civilization of Love & Tolerance* (New Jersey: The Light Inc., 2004), 36.

3. Gülen, *Love & Tolerance*, 58.

4. Fethullah Gülen, *Pearls of Wisdom* (Somerset, NJ: The Light Inc., 2000), 75.

5. Ibid.

6. Gülen, *Love & Tolerance*, 75–76.

7. Ibid., 31.

8. Ibid., 42.

9. Gülen, *Love & Tolerance*, 27–30.

10. Ibid., 61.

CHAPTER 9

1. C. S. Lewis, *Mere Christianity* (New York: HarperOne, 2000), 35.

2. See the excellent biography of C. S. Lewis by Alistair McGrath, *C. S. Lewis— A Life: Eccentric Genius, Reluctant Prophet* (Tyndale House, 2013).

3. I am indebted to my colleague Dr. Michael Ward for his insights in this chapter. For more, consult his essay "The Good Serves the Better and Both the Best: C. S. Lewis on Imagination and Reason in Apologetics," pp. 59–78, in *Imaginative Apologetics: Theology, Philosophy and the Catholic Tradition*, ed. Andrew Davison (Grand Rapids: Baker Academic, 2011), 65.

4. C. S. Lewis, "Myth Became Fact," in *God in the Dock: Essays on Theology and Ethics* (Grand Rapids: Eerdmans, 1971), 64.

5. Michael Ward, "The Good Serves the Better," 68.

6. Roger Olson, *The Mosaic of Christian Belief: Twenty Centuries of Unity & Diversity* (Downers Grover, IL: InterVarsity, 2002), 77.

7. Lewis, *Mere Christianity*, p. 35.

CONCLUSION

1. C. S. Lewis, *Mere Christianity* (New York: HarperOne, 2000), 8.

ABOUT THE AUTHOR

David Capes is the Thomas Nelson Research Professor at Houston Baptist University. He is a noted Pauline scholar, and he is the senior Bible scholar for The Voice™ Bible translation. He is the author and editor of several books, including *The Voice of Hebrews*, *Old Testament Yahweh Texts in Paul's Christology*, *Rediscovering Paul*, and *Thriving in Babylon*. He is co-host of the weekly radio show "A Show of Faith" on 1070 AM KNTH. David and his wife Cathy have three sons and one grandson.

REFRACTION

GOD ALIGNS PEOPLE OF FAITH TO HIS PURPOSES

Thomas Nelson's Refraction collection of books offer biblical responses to the biggest issues of our time, topics that have been tabooed or ignored in the past. The books will give readers insights into these issues and what God says about them, and how to respond to others whose beliefs differ from ours in a transparent and respectful way. Refraction books cross theological boundaries in an open and honest way, through succinct and candid writing for a contemporary, millenial-minded reader.

LEARN MORE AT REFRACTIONBOOKS.COM

ALSO AVAILABLE